CONTENTS

LEAH, THE AFRICAN LIONESS

Leah lies in the dappled sunlight, her tawny body stretched out.
Her three cubs play nearby. Leah is an African lioness,
and she is safe and secure with her pride.

Close by stands the majestic Pantha, the pride's dominant male.
He looks out over the savannah, watching both for food
and for danger. Pantha is the father of Leah's cubs,
and it is his responsibility to keep the whole group safe.

The pride is quite small – just Leah, her four sisters,
Pantha and his second-in-command (a younger male)
and six cubs. Leah's three cubs are just eight weeks
old and still drink her milk. Sometimes Leah suckles
her sister's three cubs, too.

ANIMAL STORY

LIONESS SUMMER

by Dougal Dixon

With thanks to our consultant: Tricia Holford, from the Born Free Foundation

ticktock

ANIMAL STORY

LIONESS SUMMER

Copyright © ticktock Entertainment Ltd 2004
First published in Great Britain in 2004 by ticktock Media Ltd.,
Unit 2, Orchard Business Centre, North Farm Road, Tunbridge Wells, Kent, TN2 3XF
We would like to thank: Jean Coppendale and Elizabeth Wiggans.
ISBN 1 86007 524 X pbk
Printed in China
A CIP catalogue record for this book is available from the British Library.

The cubs playfully stalk and pounce on the black tuft at the end of Leah's twitching tail. For now, they do not need to worry about their food. But when they are adults, they will have to hunt for themselves. Chasing tails is good hunting practise for the future!

Leah and her pride live on the grasslands of Africa. In the wet season, torrential rain sweeps across the savannah. In the dry season, the landscape can be as dry as a desert.

Yellow grasses stretch away to the horizon, with bushes and thorn trees dotted here and there.

The grasslands are home to vast herds of hoofed animals. The wildebeest, antelope and zebra that live here have adapted to this environment, and can digest the tough grass. They graze on the plains, migrating from place to place to find the best food. Small groups of giraffe feed from the thorn trees and warthogs snuffle at the earth, rooting out the juicy underground grass stems.

The herds of grassland animals are the prey of Leah and her pride. The lions are not the only hunters in this area though. Cheetahs chase speeding antelopes, while a solitary leopard drags his meal of warthog up into a tree for safekeeping.

Packs of yapping spotted hyenas wait to make a kill, or for the chance to scavenge some food.

LIFE IN THE PRIDE

Darkness has fallen and the air is cooler. It is time to hunt.

The six cubs are left with one of the females, while two of the lionesses stalk out into the darkness, silently circling a group of zebra. Leah and her other sister move into position, ready to ambush their prey. The scent of the two female lions is carried on the breeze towards the uneasy herd. As soon as the zebra detect the smell, they know it means danger. They stampede away from the two females. This is exactly what the pride wanted them to do. Snorting and panicking, the herd of zebra run straight into Leah and her other sister, waiting motionless in the long grass.

Leah suddenly leaps, dragging
a passing zebra into the dusty soil.
She seizes it by the neck, her strong
jaw and huge teeth crushing the life from
her victim. The hunt is a success.

The two male lions move in to begin the feast,
while the hungry lionesses and cubs wait for
their turn to eat.

When the family are not hunting or relaxing, Pantha patrols the boundaries of their home range.

He makes sure that no other males try to take over their territory by leaving his scent on the trees and rocks, and by making claw marks in the trunks of the trees. At sunset, his huge territorial roar can be heard across the plains, telling other lions in the area to stay away.

Pantha is an impressive sight. He is larger and heavier than his females, with his thick mane making him look even bigger. Pantha has been leading the pride for four years. But he is getting old. His eyesight is failing and he is becoming slower.

One evening, while away from the rest of the pride, Pantha suddenly finds himself surrounded by a pack of spotted hyenas.

The hyenas circle around Pantha, coming at him from all sides. Distracting him here. Biting him there.

There is nothing he can do. Pantha is doomed.

Back at the pride, Leah and her sisters sense that something is wrong. They sniff the night air. Where is their leader?

A NEW LEADER

It is as if the news has spread out across the plains. Leah's pride is without a leader. By the next day, there is a stranger prowling around their territory.

A new male has appeared – a large, fierce lion covered in scars from fighting. The young male in Leah's pride does not stand a chance, and he is driven away by the newcomer.

Now the pride's cubs are in great danger. When a new male takes over a pride, he wants the pride to be his, he does not want to take charge of another male's cubs.

Within hours the new male has killed Leah's sister's cubs. The shocked lioness paws at the little bodies of her babies, but there is no movement and no purring noises. Without these signs of life, she soon loses interest. In a few days she will have completely forgotten her cubs, and will be ready to mate with the new dominant male.

But Leah is not so easily controlled. She bravely fights face-to-face with the new male, snarling and pawing the air as soon as he comes close to her babies. After a while, the huge male gives in. Leah's cubs will survive the takeover.

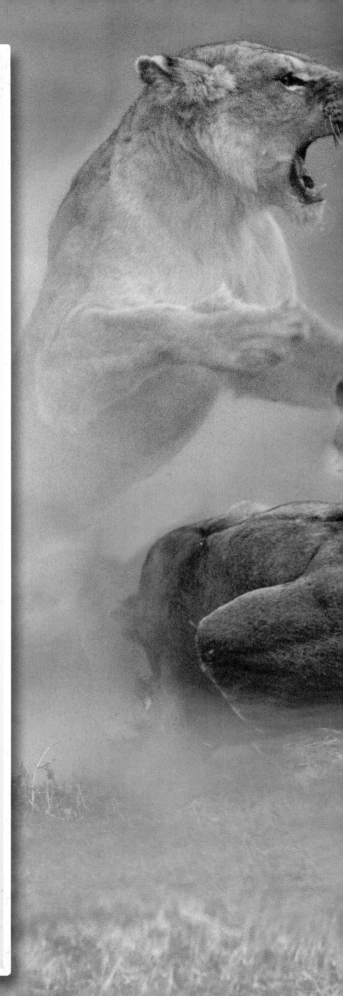

It is the end of the dry season, and prey is hard to find. However, soon the rains will come and fresh, new grass will grow. Then the herds of wildebeest, antelope and zebra will return to Leah's territory.

But this year when the rains come, the herds do not. The new dominant male is good at searching out prey, but something is keeping the herds away.

When there is plenty of food, lions only need to hunt every few days. But now Leah leads the other lionesses out day after day, with little success. Hunger is beginning to set in.

Then one morning several strange lionesses approach Leah's pride. They look hungry too. The strangers circle closer and closer, but Leah is not afraid. When she fought with the new male, she established herself as the dominant female in the pride. Now, she attacks the strangers, and the rest of the pride follow her lead.

The newcomers realize that they are not welcome and move on. But Leah and her family are unsettled. Strange lions are trying to move into their territory and, even though it is the rainy season, the herds of wildebeest and antelope have still not come.

Day after day, the hungry pride peer out from the dripping grass, over the empty savannah.

TROUBLE ON THE SAVANNAH

Time is running out. Leah and her family will have to travel farther afield to search for food.

As the lions roam across the deserted, wet grassland, they come across something they have never seen before.

A deep canyon has been excavated. There are huge machines, loud rumbling noises – and humans. A mining company is looking for valuable minerals and metals in the ground, and hundreds of men are working here. Hunters and trappers have been sent out onto the plain to catch animals to feed the men. The migrating herds of wildebeest and antelope have been scared away.

e workers have brought their own food, too. In a large pen there is a herd of cattle. e pride watches from a distance. Leah has never seen cattle before. But to a hungry ness with starving cubs, they look like prey.

The pride waits. As the sun begins to set, the men stop their work and go into the temporary buildings and tents around their camp.

Leaving the cubs to be looked after by one of the females, the pride creep into the camp. They sniff about and look at all the strange new things. But the lions are not really interested in the tools and trucks that the people have brought with them.

They only want to get to the cattle in the pen.

The fence is strong enough to keep the cattle in, but it is not high enough to keep the hungry lions out.

One by one, the lions leap the fence and land among the cattle. But it is a clumsy attack. Hungry lions do not plan well, especially against prey they have never hunted before. The cattle panic, making a terrible noise. Leah and the others leap and lunge, and several of the smaller cattle are killed.

But the lions do not have time to eat. The noise and confusion has alerted the men. Lights come on around the camp, and suddenly the air is full of shouting and guns firing. Leah and her family flee. Still hungry.

THE PRIDE MUST ESCAPE

*The miners are angry at the loss of their cattle.
Leah and her pride are hungrier than ever,
and now they are in serious danger.*

From the camp the men come, with flaming torches,
tracker dogs and guns. The men want to make
sure that they are not disturbed by lions again.

Leah watches from a rocky outcrop. Even if the
men were not carrying torches, with her excellent
night vision, she would still be able to see them
approaching across the open plain. Now the dogs
have picked up the lions' scent and are howling
and straining at their leashes. Leah fears for
her cubs. She turns and leads her babies
and the other lionesses away.

However, the male lion does not retreat. He stands his ground. As the humans approach, he charges at them. The male lion expects the group of men to act the way that herds of antelope and zebra do – panic and flee. But it does not happen. The men have guns.

The male does not return to the pride.

In many parts of Africa lions and humans now compete for space as farming and industry take over the lions' natural habitat.

Without the grassland, the herds of zebra, wildebeest and antelope disappear. Desperate lions are sometimes forced to attack the cattle on farms.

Now that the humans have taken over Leah's old territory, there is danger there and not enough food. Leah and her pride will have to move on.

On the first day of a long trek, the lionesses manage to catch a warthog. It is good meat, but it does not go far between five lionesses and three cubs.

After several days, the pride come across a few small herds of antelope. It looks like a good place to stop, but there is already a pride of lions living here. The other lions are determined to hold on to their territory. Leah and her family are forced to move on.

At a waterhole, the tired lionesses and exhausted cubs stop for a drink. But elephants are bathing there with their calves. Lions are not a danger to an adult elephant, but the herd will not risk the lions getting close to their young. The angry elephants charge, and Leah and her family are forced to flee.

A NEW LIFE

Slowly the landscape around the pride changes. The grasses become shorter as the land rises into rolling hills. Farther on, the hills become mountains.

It is very unusual for a family of lions to travel like this, but their old territory can no longer support them. Leah must find somewhere new for her pride to live.

Then, early one morning as the mist clears, the pride find themselves on a vast plain. Yellow grasses wave in the morning breeze. In the distance, they see some familiar moving shapes – herds of antelope and zebra, and giraffes nibbling from scattered thorn trees. This place looks like home.

Leah does not know it, but her pride will be safe here. They have crossed over a special border laid out by humans. They are now in a wildlife reserve.

*Leah lies in the dappled sunlight,
her tawny body stretched out.
Her three new cubs play nearby.*

Leah's hungry babies who made the long trek with her that summer, have grown up. Leah's daughter is sleeping nearby, but her two sons have left the pride. They now live with several other young males in a small bachelor group. One day they will lead prides of their own.

In the last 18 months, Leah's group has settled into life on the wildlife reserve. Eventually, two new males joined the pride and, when her original cubs no longer needed her, Leah mated with the dominant male.

Now the family sleep for up to 20 hours each day and hunt together at night, taking prey from the plentiful herds of hoofed animals that live on the reserve. The only humans that come here are tourists with cameras, or farmers who understand that they need to share the reserve with the lions.

Leah and her pride are safe and secure in their new territory.

LION FACT FILE

Lions are members of the felidae, or cat family. The lion's scientific name is *Panthera* Leo (*Panthera* is lion in Greek and *leo* is lion in Latin). Two subspecies of African lion, the Barbary lion and the Cape lion are now extinct, and the Asiatic lion (from Asia) is critically endangered.

THE WORLD OF THE AFRICAN LION

African lions are found in the areas marked on the map. Lion populations living in protected wildlife reserves are doing well. Elsewhere in Africa, lions only exist in small numbers and these populations are in danger of disappearing.

HABITAT

- Lions live on the African savannah. Their main habitat is among the scatterings of trees and bushes on the savannah.

- Lions share their world with other large carnivores, such as cheetahs, leopards and hyenas.

- The African grasslands support vast herds of prey animals, such as zebra, wildebeest, antelope and buffalo. The herds migrate from place-to-place to find the most lush areas of grass.

- In the dry season (the winter), the plant-life dies off. In the rainy season (the summer), the plant-life bursts back into life.

- Unlike most plants that grow from the tip, grass stems grow from the base. This means that when the grass is eaten by animals or damaged by dry weather conditions or fire, it can regrow.

Lions are found in the west of Africa in Cameroon, Nigeria and Senegal.

Healthy lion populations can be found in protected areas in South Africa, Botswana, Namibia, Zambia, Zimbabwe, Mozambique, Tanzania, Kenya, Uganda, Ethiopia and the east of Sudan.

PHYSICAL CHARACTERISTICS

FEMALE

Length: up to 2.5 metres
(including tail)

Average weight:
up to 180 kilograms

MALE

Length: 2 – 3 metres
(including tail)

Average weight:
up to 240 kilograms

- A male lion's mane helps to make him look larger and more impressive to other males. It may also help to protect his throat during fights.

- A male's mane begins to grow when he is about two years old.

- All lions have a black tuft of hair at the end of their tail.

- Lions have little dots on their muzzles, around their whiskers. The dots stay the same throughout the lion's life and are as individual as your fingerprints.

- Cubs are born with a slightly spotty coat. The spots begin to fade when they are about three months old.

- In the wild, lions can live for about 15 to 18 years. However, most of them only live for about 5 to 10 years.

AFRICAN GRASSLANDS FOOD WEB

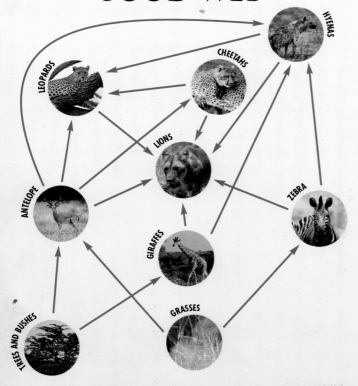

This food web shows how the animals and plants living on the African grasslands depend on each other for food. The arrows in the web mean 'give food to'.

DIET

- The lion's main diet includes wildebeest, zebra, antelope and warthogs. They will catch small animals such as hares, too!

- Lions hunt using teamwork – stalking, surrounding and ambushing their prey. Sometimes a group of lions working together will catch a really big animal, such as a buffalo.

- Lions obtain their food both by hunting and by scavenging, or stealing meat from other carnivores.

- Only about 30% of a pride's hunts are successful!

- A lion can eat as much as 27 kilograms of meat in one go! A normal meal is about 7 kilograms.

- After a hunt, the males get to eat first, then the lionesses and finally the cubs.

- Lions will eat their whole kill in one go, but may then not eat again for a few days.

- Lions lap up water with their tongues, but only a little at a time. It can take a lion up to ten minutes to quench its thirst.

BEHAVIOUR AND SENSES

- Lions are the only cats that live in large multi-female groups.

- Prides can be as small as three members or as large as 50. Most prides have about 15 members.

- All the lionnesses in a pride are normally related: sisters, daughters, mothers and grandmothers.

- Males leave the pride when they are two to four years old. Brothers will normally stick together for life and join up with other males to form bachelor groups. Each bachelor group will have its own territory and will work as a team to defend it.

- A male lion may only stay in charge of his pride for about two to fours years before a new dominant male, or male coalition, takes over, and he is forced out.

- To mark the boundary of their territory, lions will leave scratch marks on tree trunks, and rub scent and spray urine on bushes and trees.

- The adult members of a pride will happily let cubs pull at their fur and chase their tails — even the dominant male. This behaviour allows the cubs to practise skills that they will need when they are hunting as adults.

- Lions cannot see colour as well as humans, but they can see in the dark six times better than you!

- A male lion's roar can be heard 8 kilometres away!

- Lions sleep and rest for up to 20 hours each day, mainly hunting when it is dark and cool. Their hunting is not always successful, so this lifestyle allows them to save energy.

- Lions can run at 58 km/h over short distances.

REPRODUCTION AND YOUNG

- Females are pregnant for about 14 to 15 weeks. Unless their cubs die, they will not have another litter for about two and a half years.

- If her cubs are killed, a female will want to mate again within about four days.

- On average, two to four cubs are born in each litter.

- Newborn cubs weigh about 1 to 2 kilograms.

- Females give birth in a 'den site' (among thick grasses or bushes, or in a rocky outcrop). The mother introduces the cubs to the rest of the pride when they are about four to six weeks old.

- Cubs drink their mother's milk until they are about six to eight months old. They begin to eat meat when they are about six weeks old.

- Cubs are dependent on their mother until they are about 16 months old.

- Females in a pride often give birth to their cubs around the same time. The babies grow up together and are cared for in a sort of 'cub nursery'.

- Like other cats, lionesses carry their cubs in their mouths.

GLOSSARY

ADAPTED When the bodies and lifestyles of a species of animal have changed, over a very long period in time, so that they are just right for the environment where they live.

AMBUSH To wait and then attack from a hidden position.

DOMINANT MALE The lead male in a family or group of animals. Normally the largest and strongest male who has won his position by fighting off rivals. In lion prides, the dominant male fathers all the cubs.

GRASSLANDS Dry areas where the only plants that will grow are tough grasses.

MIGRATING When animals move from one area to another during different seasons of the year. Animals migrate to find new food supplies, to breed or to move to warmer places during the winter.

SAVANNAH Grasslands where some trees and bushes grow. At some times of the year they are very dry and at others there is lots of rain. Savannah grasslands are normally warm all year round.

SCAVENGE When an animal eats other animals' leftovers or carrion (animals that are already dead).

STALK To follow without being seen.

SUBMISSIVE When an animal is willing to give in to another animal, who is stronger or more dominant.

WILDLIFE RESERVES (protected areas) In some African countries vast areas are now protected by law as special wildlife reserves or protected areas (parks). Wild animals live in these areas and are protected from hunters by wardens.

In protected areas of grassland, the organizations who look after the area make sure that there is enough grassland to feed large herds of prey animals such as zebra and antelope. The herds provide food for predator animals such as lions. Some farming is allowed, but the farmers have to make sure that they leave enough land for the wild animals, and keep their own cattle well protected – so that lions and other big cats are not tempted to hunt them! Tourists pay to visit the parks to watch and photograph the animals. This helps to bring in extra money for the local villages.

CONSERVATION

- Lions once lived wild in Africa, Asia and southern Europe.

- The critically endangered Asiatic lion lives only in the Gir Forest National Park in India. There are fewer than 300 left!

- There are between 17,000 and 23,000 lions living wild in Africa.

- In many places in Africa lions are losing their natural habitat as farmland and towns expand. The large herds of prey animals that the lions rely on for food disappear, and the lions turn to farm animals as a source of food. Many lions are shot by farmers.

- Lions are sometimes shot by hunters for sport. Male lions with their impressive manes are especially popular.

- There are many cases of big cats such as lions and leopards being kept in tiny cages in poorly run zoos, as pets and as attractions in circuses or night clubs. Conservation organizations are sometimes able to rescue these big cats and rehome them in special reserves or sanctuaries where they can live their lives as they would in the wild.

FIND OUT MORE

Read more about rescuing and re-homing big cats and protecting their natural habitats at: www.bornfree.org.uk

INDEX

PICTURE CREDITS

t=top, b=bottom, c=centre, l=left, r=right, OFC=outside front cover, OBC=outside back cover

Alamy: OFC, 1c, 4, 7b, 12l, 14-15, 16-17, 18, 19bl, 20-21, 22-23, 26-27t, 26-27b, OBC. Corbis: 5cl, 6l, 6lc, 8-9, 10, 11b, 13, 17tr, 19t, 24-25, 28, 29, 30, 31. Nature Picture Library: 11t.

Every effort has been made to trace the copyright holders, and we apologize in advance for any unintentional omissions. We would be pleased to insert the appropriate acknowledgements in any subsequent edition of this publication.

Part 1

Getting started

Author: John Woodthorpe

The Open University

TU100
My digital life

Block 1
Myself

The Open University
Walton Hall, Milton Keynes
MK7 6AA

First published 2011. [Second edition 2014.]

Edited and designed by The Open University.

Typeset by SR Nova Pvt. Ltd, Bangalore, India.

Printed in the United Kingdom by Latimer Trend and Company Ltd, Plymouth.

The paper used in this publication is procured from forests independently certified to the level of Forest Stewardship Council (FSC) principles and criteria. Chain of custody certification allows the tracing of this paper back to specific forest-management units (see www.fsc.org).

ISBN 978 1 7800 7919 6

2.1

Contents

Part 2 Anything, anywhere

Part 3 Building the Web

You can find this part of the block online. A link is provided on the TU100 website.

Part 4 Geography is history

You can find this part of the block online. A link is provided on the TU100 website.

Part 5 Seeing Sense

This part of the block gives you an introduction to programming using Sense and the SenseBoard. Further details are provided in the resources page associated with this part on the TU100 website.

Part 6 Wireless communications and mobile computing

You can find this part of the block online. A link is provided on the TU100 website.

Introduction

Welcome to the first part of TU100 *My digital life*. At this point you may be wondering what a digital life is, whether you have one, and just why TU100 has this title. The answers to these questions should become clearer as your study progresses but, to set the scene, I want you to start thinking about them now.

To begin, you'll need to know that a *digital technology* is any technology based on representing data as sequences of numbers. This is a fundamental idea and you will learn much more about it as you work through TU100. At this stage, however, all you need to know is that computers use digital technologies; so the term *digital life* refers to the influence of computers, in a wide variety of forms, on the world.

Activity 1 (exploratory)

To start you off on an exploration of what it means to have a digital life, a quiz entitled 'How digital is your life?' is provided on the TU100 website. Don't worry – there are no right or wrong answers to this quiz. It has been designed as a light-hearted and fun way to look at aspects of your digital life, and to gauge how these change over the course of your studies.

If you can access the TU100 website at this moment, please do so. You will find a link to the quiz in the 'Study resources' section on the left-hand side. It doesn't matter if you can't attempt it straight away, but please try to do it soon.

Comment

As I said above, there are no right or wrong answers to this quiz, so please don't worry if some of the questions don't seem relevant to you. You will return to the quiz at intervals throughout TU100, and you should see that your responses to many of the questions change as you learn about new ideas, develop new skills and become more confident in your digital life.

Over the next few months you'll experience and investigate a wide range of aspects of what it means to have a digital life. Many of the things we enjoy – such as music, pictures, email and social networking – are based on digital technologies, and you will see how advances in these technologies have led to them playing an increasingly significant role in our lives. You'll analyse examples of individuals and groups using technologies to develop friendships, to work more efficiently and to learn together. TU100 will also show you how digital technologies are used to create games and virtual worlds that we can become immersed in (sometimes to the detriment of our 'real' lives).

You will examine some practical examples, and explore some of the issues and debates that surround the use of digital technologies in a range of everyday situations. You will see how we can now communicate and share information in ways that would have been astonishing even a few decades ago. However, you will also see that the underlying principles enabling us to do this have developed gradually from ideas that have been around for a great deal longer.

Most of the uses of technology that you'll consider will be legal and harmless. However, you will also look at some examples that subvert laws and the rights of others, and some that move into the worlds of crime and terror where information is transmitted that others want to intercept, control or suppress. Effective participation in the digital world therefore requires you to become aware of many technical, social and ethical pitfalls, as well as some of the ways you can avoid them.

Throughout TU100 you will not only learn about digital technologies and their influence on our lives, but also actively use some of these technologies. You'll work with the *hardware* and programming components supplied with the materials to learn how to write simple *programs* for electronic *smart devices*, as well as how to incorporate information from the Web and from your home into these programs. As you study you will use a range of online services and resources, and you will also be part of an online community of TU100 students.

If you're interested in the technologies used in work environments, or in pursuing a career in computing or communication technologies, TU100 will show you how you can explore the range of roles that exist, identify the skills and knowledge needed for such positions, and decide how you might progress in your career.

Not everyone studying TU100 will be intending to take further modules in this subject area. If you are one of those who are, the TU100 website will be used to indicate some of the options open to you and give an idea of the modules you might take. If your interests lie in the less technical aspects of TU100, the module team will give you reasons for working through material you might find less relevant by showing you how the technology it introduces has changed all our lives.

My job in this first part of TU100 is to start you off on the digital journey that you'll be making over the next few months. You will learn a little about the historical development of computers and their role in today's society, and you will consider examples of digital technologies in the world around you and their influence on your life. However, this part merely introduces some of the key ideas; you will study them, and others not mentioned here, in greater depth later on.

Some of the things you study over the next few months may be familiar to you, but others will be new. I hope that you find most, if not all, of them interesting and enjoyable.

Don't forget to make entries in your learning journal after each study session or at the end of the part, as described in the *TU100 Guide* – you may find it useful to return to your initial thoughts when you come to study each topic in more detail.

Learning outcomes

As described in the *TU100 Guide*, learning outcomes express what you are expected to gain from studying TU100, both in terms of understanding concepts and in terms of developing skills. Below are the learning outcomes related to this part; however, you should note that all of these areas will be developed further as your study of TU100 progresses.

Your study of this part will help you to do the following.

Knowledge and understanding

- Understand the concept of a 'digital life'.
- Be aware of the role of information and communication technologies in a digital life.
- Be aware of some of the hardware, software and communication components used in information and communication technologies.

Key skills

- Develop skills in taking notes.
- Develop study skills at a level appropriate to higher education, such as study planning, learning from feedback and reading actively.
- Keep a learning journal.

Practical and professional skills

- Interact with others at a distance using communication technologies.
- Work collaboratively online with other students, applying principles of netiquette.

Computers: from novelty to commonplace

1

The theme of this session is the development of digital technologies, from the physically large and highly expensive equipment of the 1950s to the omnipresent networks and computer-based devices upon which our digital lives are founded today. In this session I will:

- compare the development of the computer to the development of the telephone
- describe some of the digital technologies that form an integral part of many of our lives
- introduce the term *information society*.

Timings
This is the first study session in Part 1. It should take you around one hour to complete.

1.1 The telephone

In the 1950s, telephones represented the cutting edge of technology (Figure 1). However, they were not only large and expensive to purchase but also inconvenient to use; if you wanted to make a call over a distance of more than fifteen miles, you had first to call the operator who would then make the connection.

Telephones were also expensive to use. In the UK calls were charged in units of three minutes, each unit costing the equivalent of between 5 and 20 pence in today's currency. (In comparison, in 1959 a pint of milk cost about 3 pence.) Few people had a home telephone and even fewer made long-distance calls. The high cost of using a telephone ensured that anyone who had one tended to use it infrequently, and then only for short calls.

Figure 1   A 1950s telephone

In 1959 the General Post Office, which ran almost all UK telephone systems at the time, introduced subscriber trunk dialling (STD). This advance in technology allowed users to make long-distance calls directly, without an operator, and to be charged only for the actual duration of the call. The telephone became easier and much cheaper to use; as a result, more people began to use it and for longer calls.

Over time the telephone has become part of the background of our lives, until today it is extremely unusual to find someone who has neither a home telephone nor a mobile phone. Just as the telephone changed from a status symbol to become simply another piece of the modern world, so the computer is making a similar transition.

1.2   The computer

There were very few computers in the 1950s, and those in existence were treated as objects of wonder with almost mythical powers. They were nothing like the computers of today, as you'll see in a later part. For one thing they were huge, with the refrigerator-sized one shown in Figure 2 being relatively small for the time. They were also delicate, and consumed a lot of electricity, wasting much of it as heat.

Nowadays, however, a computer is just another item stocked in supermarkets alongside toothpaste and dog food. And as computers have become cheaper and smaller, they have been incorporated into a kaleidoscopic range of devices that bear no resemblance to what was once thought of as a computer. Powerful computers now sit at the heart of objects as diverse as mobile phones and games consoles, cars and vacuum cleaners. The cost of computer power continues to decrease, making it possible to incorporate computer technologies into almost any object, no matter how small, cheap or disposable. And these smart devices are

Figure 2   A 1950s computer

'talking' to one another, not just within a single room or building but across the world via the *internet*, using the *World Wide Web* (see Box 1). Thus even as the computer vanishes from sight, it becomes vastly more powerful and ever-present – to use a term you'll become very familiar with, it is now *ubiquitous*.

Activity 2 (exploratory)

Can you think of another technology that has made the transition from novel to commonplace, like telephones and computers?

Comment

There are many possible answers to this question. I thought of washing machines, which have advanced from hand-driven drums to the automatic machines of today.

1.3   The information society

Networks and the internet

As a result of advances in *information and communication technology (ICT)*, our notions of time and location are changing – distance is no longer a barrier to commercial or social contact for those of us connected to suitable *networks*. Some people may find it difficult to imagine not having access to the information and services that play a crucial part in their daily lives. Others may feel that they have no part to play in the

Box 1   The internet and the Web

You will come across the terms *internet* and *Web* a lot in TU100. Although in everyday life people tend to use these terms interchangeably, in reality they are two separate (though related) entities.

The internet is a global network of networks: an *internetwork* (hence its name). It is the infrastructure that connects computers together. At first written with an upper-case 'I', it is increasingly seen with a lower-case 'i'.

The Web (short for *World Wide Web*), on the other hand, is a service that links files across computers, allowing us to access and share information. Thus the Web is a software system that has been built upon the hardware of the internet.

Apart from anything else, this means that it is technically incorrect to refer to 'searching' or 'browsing' the internet. When you carry out an online search, you are in fact searching the Web!

digital world because their network access is very limited or even non-existent. Some simply don't care about the digital world, viewing it perhaps as a waste of time. Yet whether we are aware of it or not, digital information is flowing constantly around us.

Consider a computer that is connected to the internet – the one you intend to use in studying TU100, for example. This may be a computer you use at home, in a library or at work; you may use it on the move or in a fixed location. Whatever the case, this computer is part of a complex system consisting of wires and optical fibres, microwaves and lasers, switches and satellites, that encompasses almost every part of the world. The oceans are wrapped in more than a quarter of a million miles of fibre-optic *cable* with several strands of glass running through it. Each of these strands can carry thousands of simultaneous telephone conversations, a few dozen television channels, or any of a range of other forms of digital content (such as web pages).

This modern communications network enables us to use a mobile phone in the depths of Siberia or take a satellite telephone to the Antarctic (Figure 3), watch television in the middle of the Atlantic, do our banking from an airliner, or play games with a person on the other side of the world. It is one of the greatest technological achievements of the last thirty years and it is so reliable, so omnipresent, that we very rarely stop to think about what actually happens when we dial a telephone number, click on a web link or switch TV channels. Or rather, we tend not to think about it until something disrupts the network – whether it be a widespread problem such as a power cut, or something more localised such as finding ourselves in a rural area with no mobile phone signal.

The end of the twentieth century and the beginning of the twenty-first century are often compared to other historical periods of great change, such as the Industrial Revolution, because of the huge technological changes that are happening in many areas of our lives. These

Figure 3   Using a satellite phone in the Antarctic

developments are taking place in conjunction with correspondingly large social and economic changes, often characterised by the terms *information society* and *network society*. Such notions are frequently referred to by policy makers when driving forward changes in our technological infrastructure: politicians often refer to the inevitability of technological change in our information society and stress the need to be at the forefront of these changes in order to secure future prosperity, for example by developing broadband network infrastructure, by making public services available online, and by equipping schools and local communities with computers.

Activity 3 (exploratory)

Can you think of an example where changes in technology have resulted in changes to your work, social or family life? Have those changes improved your life? Have they created any problems?

Comment

The biggest change for me has been in my ability to work from home. I'm currently sitting at home typing this text on a computer whilst listening to some jazz music, which is also stored on the computer. I'll shortly email my document to a colleague, who will be able to read it a few seconds later.

My first job required me to travel to my employer's premises every day and share an office – and a single telephone – with ten other people. When I needed to write a report I would do it with a pen and paper for someone else to type up. A few days later I'd get it back to check and the typist would make any corrections with something called 'correcting fluid'.

Being able to work from home has improved my life considerably. Not only does it save me the time and money that used to be spent on travelling, but being able to listen to music while I work helps me concentrate, as well as making the job more enjoyable. On the down side, the boundaries between my home life and my work life have become very blurred, as my wife will confirm. So on the whole I feel the changes are positive, but there are some disadvantages as well.

The rise of texting

Unintended uses sometimes develop alongside the intended uses of emerging technologies in our information society. A classic example is the text messaging facility on mobile phones, often referred to as *SMS* (which stands for short message service). This was originally a minor feature designed to be used by engineers testing equipment – it was not expected to be used by phone owners at all. Yet by 2006, mobile phone companies were earning more than 80 billion US dollars per year worldwide from SMS messages, making them one of the most profitable parts of their business (International Telecommunication Union, 2006).

SMS resulted in a whole new method of communication and form of popular culture, different ways of interacting with radio and television, and even a new language form: texting. Texting often plays a key role in arranging demonstrations against those in power. You will probably remember such events from recent news stories, and you'll look at the role this sort of technology can play in protest movements in a later part.

Some more figures might help to put the increase in texting into context. The Mobile Data Association gathers statistics on mobile phone usage in the UK. Their report for May 2008 (Text.it, 2008) shows that in the whole of that month:

- 16.5 million people accessed the internet from their mobile phones
- 6.5 billion SMS (text) messages were sent
- both of these figures showed a considerable increase from previous years.

In December 2008, the equivalent figures were 17.4 million and 7.7 billion respectively. In the following activity you will calculate just how large the increase in text messaging between May and December was.

> 'Billion' is a word that in the past had different meanings in the UK and the USA. However, the two countries now agree that a billion is one thousand million (1000 000 000), and TU100 will follow that convention.

The numerical exercises in TU100 are intended to help you develop your understanding of the material.

Activity 4 (self-assessment)

The number of text messages sent per month in the UK grew from 6.5 billion in May 2008 to 7.7 billion in December 2008. What was the percentage growth over those seven months? You will probably need to use a calculator for this activity.

Note: as in all the printed parts of TU100, answers to self-assessment activities may be found at the end of the part. If your maths skills are a bit rusty then you may wish to refer to the resources page associated with this part on the TU100 website, which provides links to information on various mathematical concepts, including percentages and how to use a calculator.

1.4   Conclusion

In this session, having briefly considered the rapid development of computers, I outlined some of the ways in which digital technologies pervade the world around us, giving rise to the social and economic changes that characterise our information society. The concept of an information society is a key one in TU100, and in the next session I'll try to give you a better idea of what it involves.

2 Some aspects of our information society

Timings

This is the second study session in Part 1. It should take you around three hours to complete. If you don't have time to work through it all at once, there are break points where you can stop and return later.

ubiquitous – being present every where at once.

In the previous session I introduced the concept of an information society; in this session I will outline some key aspects of such a society. Many of the ideas you meet here will reappear several times during your study of TU100.

The changeable nature of the online world

One of the things you will notice while studying TU100 is that some of the examples you read about no longer exist, or are nothing like as important as when the material was written in 2010 and 2011. This is inevitable, and you shouldn't be concerned by it; your focus should be on the general principles, which remain valid.

As an example, there was a time when if you wanted to find something online you didn't go to Google, because that didn't exist. Instead, you almost certainly went to a search engine called AltaVista. I've just checked and this currently still exists at http://www.altavista.com, but it is now owned by Yahoo! and looks very similar to Google. However, back in the late 1990s it was seen as the definition of what a community *portal* site should be, combining a search function with links to a range of information sources; as a result, it was the first-choice search engine for many people. It continued to develop, and was one of the first to allow users to search for images and to translate text from one language to another. However, by late 2001 Google had overtaken AltaVista in both popularity and ease of use, and we've now reached the stage where relatively few internet users use or even know about AltaVista.

The same sort of thing will happen as you study TU100. Some companies you read about may no longer exist, and some may be more or less prominent. Yet the likelihood is that although companies come and go, there will still be ways to share photos (as Flickr and Picasa allow at the moment), to edit documents online (as is possible with Microsoft Office Live and Google Docs), to store files online (as Dropbox and Ubuntu One allow), and so on.

2.1 Business

Financial services

Every time you use a debit or credit card in a shop, the shop till communicates with a card terminal that transmits your identification details from your card to your bank or credit card company for verification. Your balance is then adjusted according to your purchase. A similar chain of events is initiated if you shop online (buying a ticket for an airline or train, perhaps) or over the phone (when booking a cinema ticket, for example). Many banks also provide online banking services, reducing the need for customers to visit a branch. *Automated teller machines (ATMs)* allow you to check your bank balance and withdraw cash wherever you are in the world. In each of the above situations – using a debit or credit card, shopping or managing your money online or over the phone, or using an ATM – the machines involved are connected via a network to a central computer, which has records of your account in an electronic filing system known as a *database*.

Financial services have undergone huge changes in recent years as a result of developments in the digital technologies driving them. The examples just described show how convenient and accessible such services have become. Yet at the same time, issues of identity and security have become a concern. New ways of communicating have also created new types of crime, including identity theft and financial fraud. In turn, these problems have fostered the development of new security industries that try to inform us and sell us solutions to reduce the chances of us becoming victims of online crime.

Commerce

Advances in digital technologies have led to changes in many areas of commerce, with some existing kinds of business being transformed by the opportunities these developments offer. One of the most obvious changes is the emergence of retailers such as Amazon, which have an online shop but no physical one that customers can visit. Yet the internet not only benefits the largest companies, but also allows even the smallest retailers to advertise their services to a global audience. Incredibly specialised companies can flourish by relying on the internet's immense reach to deliver potential customers.

Of course, this growth has resulted in casualties in traditional (sometimes called 'bricks and mortar') retailing. High-street shops specialising in items such as books, DVDs, music and games have all lost business to online retailers. This has driven some shops out of business, but a number of high-street stores have also opened successful online stores. Online retailers have lower costs – they don't pay expensive high-street rents and can easily be based in countries with low tax regimes – and they can pass these savings on to customers.

Figure 4   A light-hearted look at the pros and cons of online tracking

Although the low costs offered by online stores can be very attractive to customers, they might be counterbalanced to some extent by the less immediate and less tangible nature of the shopping experience. However, online retailers make up for this by providing a variety of services that reassure and inform their customers. One such service is the tracking of goods online – though this is a development that can produce its own frustrations, as illustrated by the cartoon in Figure 4. Having bought a new computer a few years ago and tracked it on its way from the factory in China to my home, I can identify with the feeling expressed!

Activity 5 (exploratory)

Add some more entries to the following table of advantages and disadvantages of online shopping. Can you think of ways in which online retailers may try to address the disadvantages?

	Advantages	Disadvantages
Buyer	More choice	
	Can often track goods	
Seller		

Comment

I thought of the following, but you may have come up with others.

	Advantages	Disadvantages
Buyer	More choice	Can't try goods (e.g. shoes, clothes) first
	Can often track goods	Harder to return goods if faulty
	Often cheaper than a local shop	Harder to get help and advice before or after buying
	Some items can be downloaded immediately after buying	May be worried about online fraud
Seller	No need for a physical shop	Reliant on delivery services
	Lower running costs	Likely to get more returned goods
	Don't need to keep everything in stock – can arrange delivery from suppliers	Need to respond to email or telephone queries
	Can supply music, books, software, etc. for download rather than having to supply a physical item	Some potential customers reluctant to buy online

Online retailers may try to address the disadvantages listed above in various ways. For instance, they might provide:

- free collection of returned items
- links to online reviews of products to help advise prospective buyers
- telephone helplines
- support forums to help customers before and after buying
- advice on how to shop safely online.

As well as direct retailing, other types of businesses have also moved online – auction sites such as eBay fall into this category. Some online businesses are less conventional, and as a result it's often harder to see how they find the money they need to survive. For example, there are many collaborative projects that produce free products including *software*, online encyclopaedias and educational resources. These often rely on volunteers contributing their time, with money being provided by advertising, sponsorship or donations.

Work

Technology has changed the way that other businesses operate too. Greater quantities of information are exchanged between numerous locations over public and private networks. Vast amounts of data are stored on computers and accessed remotely from a variety of devices. Just as individuals buy from companies online, many companies now sell to each other online as well, for the same reasons of reduced cost and wider choice that attract individuals to online stores. Manufacturing tasks that used to take days can now be completed in minutes using computer-operated machine tools working in automated production lines.

The way we use technology has also affected our individual working lives. For example, telephone and online banking mean that banks no longer need large numbers of counter staff, and the role of travel agents has changed as more people book their holidays directly from the vendor by going online. Some companies have responded by reducing their number of employees, while others have retrained their staff to provide more specialised services to their customers. More generally, many people working in an office environment are expected to learn how to use new software applications in order to do their jobs.

In this module you will explore some of the roles that have emerged within these industries. You will also consider the job market and how technology has resulted in changes to the recruitment process. If you are studying TU100 to improve your qualifications and progress in your career, you should find this topic particularly relevant to you.

Break point
This would be a good point to take a break if you need to do something else before returning later.

2.2   Communities

As well as revolutionising the commercial world, the internet has had an enormous impact on the way we communicate. While there are still people in many parts of the world who do not have internet access, many of us have access at home or at work. As a result we have the opportunity to communicate with others using email, *instant messaging* and *online discussion groups* (in online *forums*). Existing communities have created new ways of communicating, and new online communities have developed. *Social networking* plays an increasingly significant role in the lives of many people.

The recent pace of communication change has amazed many of us, and there is no reason to think things will slow down. The cartoon map of online communities shown in Figure 5 appeared on the Web in early 2007. Since then, the social networking site Facebook has increased in significance and size at the expense of MySpace, and micro-blogging sites such as Twitter – which allows users to post and read short messages – have appeared and grown. You'll find a much larger and updated version of this map in the resources page associated with this part on the TU100 website: it gives a feel for those changes and more, and is well worth a look.

2.3   Information

The internet has had a huge impact on the availability of information of all kinds. Material on the Web reflects widely differing viewpoints, from official news bulletins to unofficial rumours, and comes from widely differing sources, from commercial megastores to community groups. Since no individual government, company or person has control over it, the internet has paved the way to unfettered publishing of information of all kinds, raising questions about the authority and regulation of this information. As you will learn in a later part, some governments try to exert control over the information their citizens can access and create, with varying degrees of success.

2.4   Entertainment

The world of entertainment is constantly evolving as new ways of creating and distributing the media we watch and listen to are developed. Digital broadcasting has changed the way we experience television and radio, with increasingly interactive and participative programmes. Digital cameras, printers and scanners, together with desktop publishing and photo-editing software, enable greater numbers of people to experiment with image production, while online image- and video-sharing sites allow anyone with access to a relatively basic mobile phone or digital camera to share photos and videos with the rest of the online world. New digital

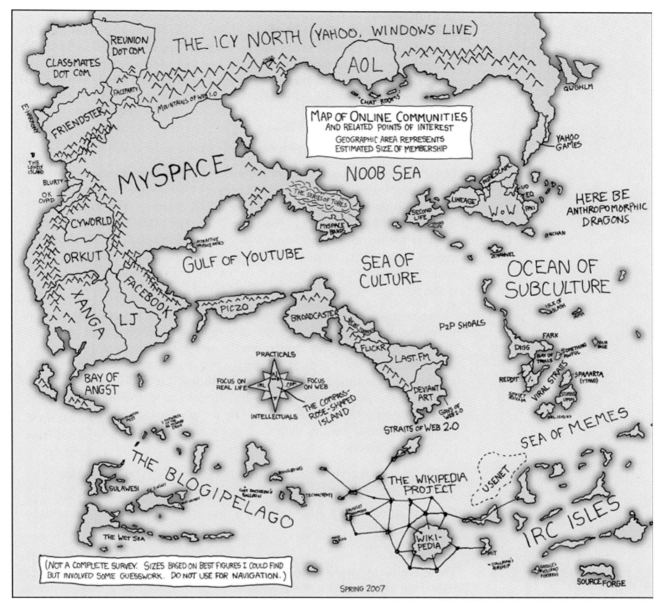

Figure 5 One view of the world's online communities in 2007: a more recent version is on the TU100 website

technologies have also been at the forefront of changes in the production and distribution of music, and computer gaming has developed hand in hand with the evolution of graphical interfaces.

However, our increased exposure to digital entertainment has resulted in increased conflict between the rights of the consumer and the rights of the producer of the media. It is now much easier for the products of the media industries established during the twentieth century – film, music and so on – to be illegally copied and distributed in a form that is indistinguishable from the original. *Copyright* holders are taking steps to prevent this by developing a range of *digital rights management (DRM)* techniques that make it much harder to create copies, as well as by trying to persuade users of the benefits of the original product. Such attempts at persuasion can look very threatening, as I noticed on a recently purchased CD that has the following printed on the back cover:

FBI Anti-piracy Warning:

Unauthorized copying is punishable under federal law.

Several questions came to mind when I read this. Does that mean I can't legally put the music onto my MP3 player? Can the US Federal Bureau of Investigation extradite and punish me (a UK citizen who bought the CD in the UK) if I do? Should I return the CD to the place I bought it from and ask for my money back? Or will I be in trouble only if I distribute copies of the CD to other people? These are all valid concerns that demonstrate some of the problems surrounding the use of copyrighted material.

There are many other issues arising from this, and it is very easy to make the digital future sound bleak. You have probably heard predictions to the effect that illegally copied media, and making information freely available on the Web, will increasingly put whole businesses and hundreds of thousands of jobs in the established media industries at risk. However, as in other areas of the digital world, there are also opportunities for these businesses if they can adapt to the new environment and modify their business models to survive and grow in different directions.

Activity 6 (exploratory)

Can you think of any other problems connected with the growth of digital entertainment?

Comment

There are many possibilities. I thought of the fact that the advent of digital television affected even those who didn't particularly welcome it – across the world, analogue signals are gradually being switched off as new digital signals are introduced. In time, everyone will have to get new digital televisions as the old analogue versions become obsolete – quite an expensive business!

You might also have thought of more technical problems, such as how to transmit the large quantities of digital data required for some forms of entertainment – video, for example – in an acceptable time and retaining acceptable quality.

2.5   Public services

Public information and services

Public bodies such as governments and transport agencies are increasingly providing services online, allowing us to organise various aspects of our daily lives more easily. These services range from simple information displays, which let us check things such as weather forecasts and transport timetables, to interactive sites that allow us to make bookings or queries.

In many parts of the world, medical records are increasingly moving away from paper and X-ray film towards becoming completely digital. This has several advantages, especially in allowing patient records to be easily shared between departments within a hospital, and sometimes more widely with doctors' surgeries and other health workers. In remote rural areas of some countries, doctors can make use of computer networks or even mobile phones to make a diagnosis if they are unable to see the patient in person. However, this is by no means universal, and even where such facilities exist they aren't always available.

Information for travellers is also increasingly being made available digitally: for example, live online updates on road congestion and public transport, and arrivals information in stations and airports. Similarly, it is becoming more and more common to book plane journeys online – in fact, some airlines now only accept online bookings and will only issue electronic tickets. Many of them strongly encourage, or even require, passengers to check in online as well.

In addition, many countries provide online access to at least some of their government services. For example, you might be able to renew or apply for a passport, book a driving test, claim benefits, or fill in your tax return online. Local authorities also provide digital information services – you might be able to reserve or renew a library book online, for instance – and there are numerous opportunities to learn online, as you will be doing on TU100.

Security and risk

The twentieth century saw a dramatic change in the role of the state in many countries. During most of the nineteenth century, an individual might only have come into contact with the state for the purposes of taxation, marriage and death; at the end of that century and the beginning of the next, however, a series of social revolutions saw the state becoming involved in our healthcare, pensions and education. Unsurprisingly, each of these developments was accompanied by a significant increase in the amount of personal information stored about every one of us. Computer technologies were developed especially to serve the enormous projects

Break point
This would be a good point to take a break if you need to do something else before returning later.

involved; IBM became a highly successful company due to its work on censuses in the USA and Europe, whilst the world's first business computer, LEO, was used for a variety of tasks including the calculation of tax tables for the British Treasury in the 1950s.

With the vast amount of personal information being held about us in various places, it is becoming increasingly important for us to be able to prove our identities – not just for travel but for other activities such as purchasing expensive or restricted items, paying bills and opening bank accounts. The UK is unusual in Europe in that (at the time of writing in 2010) it does not have a compulsory identity card system, despite the fact that identity cards were put in place during both world wars. In several countries, identity card or passport schemes are being upgraded with new *biometric* technologies such as iris or face recognition, which (perhaps rather over-ambitiously) promise to uniquely identify individuals.

As well as the personal information that we know about, there may also exist information about us of which we are unaware. Since the terrorist attacks on the USA in 2001, much of the Western world has become far more security conscious, and governments and companies alike have developed and deployed technological countermeasures. These range from smart video surveillance systems that can identify an individual in a crowd and track his or her movements, through the biometric technologies mentioned above, to the searching of databases for suspicious activity.

Activity 7 (exploratory)

Can you recall an occasion when you have been personally aware of technological security measures?

Comment

On a recent visit to the USA I went through a range of airport security screenings. In addition to having my belongings checked, I was photographed at least twice (as well as being under almost constant video surveillance in the airports), had my fingerprints scanned electronically, and was required to fill in numerous online and paper forms.

The promise is that such technologies will make us safer, but could they turn the world we live in into a society strangely reminiscent of the nightmare vision contained in George Orwell's novel *1984*?

As you've seen so far in this session, there is plenty of opportunity for digital information about each of us to be created. Some of this information we might intentionally give out ourselves – on social networking sites, for example. Other information about us may, as described above, be gathered more surreptitiously by various agencies. In general we have little control over how digital information about us is used or who receives it. We might assume that information gathered legally by a government agency, for instance, will be handled appropriately and used only for our benefit; yet there have been many examples of governments and private organisations 'losing' confidential data by transferring it insecurely. For example, in November 2008 the UK government announced that two CDs containing personal information about 25 million people had been lost by HM Revenue and Customs when they were posted to the National Audit Office. If criminals got hold of such information then there would be the risk of our identity or our money being stolen.

2.6 Communicating on the move

Advances in digital technology have, in a very short space of time, revolutionised the way many of us live our lives. Nowhere is this more evident than in our ability to communicate as we travel. Below I'll share with you a personal example that highlights some of the changes, and some of the opportunities and problems these changes have created.

In the 1980s my employers of the time set up an email account for me with a commercial email provider called CompuServe. This required me to use a *modem* to connect my computer to a telephone line and dial one of a set of specific phone numbers so that my email could be transmitted. This was fine if I was in the office, but more complicated when travelling as very few hotels made telephone sockets available to customers. As a result, my travelling kit soon contained a selection of small screwdrivers for dismantling hotel telephones, and a set of wires, crocodile clips and pliers so I could wire directly into the phone system. Of course, this was all done at my own risk and without the knowledge or approval of the hotels, and I am not recommending it!

In those days, even when I did manage to get online, email transmission was very slow and expensive. Nowadays I have a mobile phone with which I can send and pick up emails quickly and cheaply wherever I am (without the need to dismantle a fixed-line telephone!). As well as email, my phone enables me to communicate in several other ways – instant messaging and social networking, for example, not to mention voice calls. I can also use the built-in *global positioning system (GPS)* to find out where I am, and even plot my location on a website to let my friends and family see where I am (or at least see where my phone is).

This last feature was very useful when my wife and I tried to find our son's new flat for the first time, as the last mile of the journey was rather more complicated than expected. Our son could check online and see exactly where we were, and he could also talk to us and guide us to the right place. Yet a service like this also has some disadvantages – most importantly, I need to remember to turn it off if I don't want people to know where I am. A few months later, I realised on returning home after buying my wife a birthday present that the same service will have showed that I spent 20 minutes in a jeweller's shop. I don't think she noticed, or if she did she didn't allow it to spoil the surprise. However, it's not hard to imagine other circumstances in which I might not want my location to be publicised, even to my family and friends (Figure 6).

Activity 8 (exploratory)

This activity is designed to make you think about the things I've said above, and to start you using some of the online facilities available to you as an Open University student. If you follow it through, it should help you to become more aware of the digital technologies driving much of our lives.

Throughout the next week I would like you to keep a diary in your learning journal of news stories featuring digital technologies. As described in the *TU100 Guide*, you can do this in your personal blog; alternatively, you can make notes on paper or in a document on your computer. However you do it, you should also note the source of each story. You'll learn more about how to give references later, but for now just a link to an online story or a note of the date and programme or newspaper will do. You can use any factual sources – television and radio news, newspapers and magazines, the Web, and so on. Try to file each story into one of the areas discussed above:

- business
- communities
- information
- entertainment
- public services
- communicating on the move.

Comment

My answer to this activity is provided in the resources page associated with this part on the TU100 website.

"I'm tracking my husband through his GPS unit.
Right now, he's between a televised sporting
event and the refrigerator."

Figure 6   The disadvantages of GPS?

2.7 Conclusion

In this session you've learned about some of the key aspects of an information society, online social networking being one of them. In the next session I'll outline some ways in which you can participate in online discussions effectively.

3 Participating in a digital world

Timings

This is the third study session in Part 1. It should take you around two hours to complete. If you don't have time to work through it all at once, there are break points where you can stop and return later.

Previously in this part I've mentioned the rise of social networking – one aspect of our increasingly digital world. You may already communicate online to some extent in your daily life, and while studying TU100 you'll certainly do so as part of an online community of tutors and students. In particular, you'll participate in your online tutor-group forum, whose members are your tutor and all the students he or she has been allocated. In a later part you will look again at the phenomenon of online communication in a variety of forms, and analyse it in some depth.

What follows in this session is a quick guide to good practice in contributing to online discussions. It should help you to work and socialise with others online – in your studies, your social life and your working life. Much of the content is summed up by the familiar tenet known as the Golden Rule: a concept common to many ethical codes, which simply states that we should treat others as we would want them to treat us. Just as this Golden Rule is relevant to good manners – 'etiquette' – when talking face to face, so it is relevant to online communication. To help us apply it, it has been developed into guidelines for online behaviour called 'net etiquette' or, more commonly, just *netiquette*.

Netiquette is intended to make us all think about how we behave online and to make us aware of the effect our words could have on others reading them. If it seems that there are far too many rules to follow, be reassured that they aren't hard and fast commands that you must remember and obey. Netiquette does not encompass every situation you may find yourself in – it's perfectly possible to obey all the guidance below and still annoy someone – but it will give you a good foundation for your participation in online discussions.

Most of what follows is common sense and good manners. Some of it may be familiar to you, but please take time to read it – and do so especially carefully if this is your first Open University module or if you don't have much experience of using online discussion groups to work with others. There's a big difference between working in an online community and socialising online, so even if you are experienced at the latter, you should find the following material useful.

3.1 Netiquette: respecting others online

As children we quickly learn many rules about how to interact with other people. Some of these rules are common sense, such as 'don't interrupt a speaker' and 'say please and thank you', and are necessary if we are to reduce the likelihood of arguments or causing offence.

When we have a face-to-face conversation, we don't just rely on the spoken words to establish the other person's meaning; unconsciously we are also monitoring the tone of their voice, their facial expression and their body language. Telephone conversations are a little more ambiguous because we can no longer see the other person; email and online discussions are harder again, since all we have is text. It is extremely easy to misinterpret words on a page, so the writer must take great care before pressing the button that sends their message to the world.

Thank, acknowledge and support people

People can't see you nod, smile or frown as you read their messages. If they get no response, they may feel ignored and be discouraged from contributing further. Why not send a short reply to keep the conversation going? This can make a big difference in a small group setting such as a tutor-group forum. However, do bear in mind that in a large, busy forum too many messages like this could be a nuisance.

Acknowledge before differing

Before you disagree with someone, try to summarise the other person's point in your own words. Then they know you are trying to understand them and will be more likely to take your view seriously. Otherwise, you risk talking at each other rather than to each other. You should also recognise that other people are entitled to their point of view, even if you consider them to be entirely wrong.

Make clear your perspective

Try to speak personally. That means avoiding statements like 'This is the way it is …' or 'It is a fact that …'. These sound dogmatic and leave no room for anyone else's perspective. Why not start by saying 'I think …' or 'I feel …'? If you are presenting someone else's views then say so, perhaps by using a quotation and acknowledgement.

Emotions

Emotions can be easily misunderstood when you can't see faces or body language. People may not realise you are joking, and irony and satire are easily missed – all good reasons to think before you send a message. To compensate for these restrictions, early internet users came up with the idea of the smiley face – :) or :-) – which then grew into a whole family of *emoticons*.

Remember that the systems upon which many forums are based only support plain text, so you can't always rely on fonts and colours to add meaning. Even if you are using a forum that allows so-called 'rich text', it's possible that other users will be picking up messages as plain text emails or as text message alerts on their mobile phones and will not see your formatting. AND DON'T WRITE IN CAPITAL LETTERS – IT WILL COME OVER AS SHOUTING!

If you read something that offends or upsets you, it is very tempting to dash off a reply immediately. However, messages written in the heat of the moment can often cause offence themselves. It's much better to save your message as a draft and take a break or sleep on it. That gives you a chance to come back to your message when you're feeling calmer and ask yourself 'how would I feel if someone sent that message to me?'. If you decide it will make things worse then make sure you edit it before you send it.

The best advice is to try to be aware of your audience before you post. The internet is a global phenomenon; people from widely differing cultures and backgrounds may read what you write online, and what you find funny may be offensive to them. It may take time to work out what sort of 'audience' can be found in a particular forum; some are very permissive and allow almost any sort of behaviour, while most (like those at The Open University) will not tolerate bad behaviour or abuse.

Activity 9 (exploratory)

Look at the email exchange shown in Figure 7. What emotions are being expressed through smileys and typography? Would Jon and Sue still be on speaking terms if they hadn't used these devices?

Comment

In Sue's first reply to Jon she expresses her frustration by typing 'Aaaarrrgggghhhhhh', but she ends that message with a winking smiley. Jon's reply then says 'sorry' in a very small voice! Sue's final reply starts with a happy smiley to show that everything's OK. She uses a large font when she mentions the annoyingly early meeting time.

I feel sure that Jon and Sue would still be friendly after this email exchange. But I have seen email exchanges between colleagues that had the opposite effect, when the participants didn't take care about how they expressed themselves in their messages.

Moderation

Moderators are forum participants responsible for keeping order. They may have capabilities within the forum greater than those of other participants; for example, they can sometimes add new participants

From: Jon
To: Sue

Dear Sue,

I've messed up by overwriting a file you've just edited.

I think I've mended the damage, but could you check I did it right?

Jon

From: Sue
To: Jon

Aaaarrrgggghhhhhh. Don't do this to me. ;o)

From: Jon
To: Sue

Sorry.

From: Sue
To: Jon

:o))))

The page looks OK. No harm done.

I had a meeting at 8.15 yes 8.15 today so forgive me if I'm a bit grumpy.

Sue

Figure 7 **Email exchange between Jon and Sue**

and suspend people who are abusive. They also work to keep the discussions friendly and relevant to the forum. A forum with a moderator is said to be *moderated*. All Open University forums are moderated, and your tutor-group forum will be moderated by your tutor. Forums without moderators are *unmoderated* and are generally places where newcomers should tread very carefully. Moderators tend to introduce themselves early on in forum discussions, so it's usually clear whether a forum is moderated or not.

Some other advice

- Keep to the subject, and pick the right forum for your contribution.
- Before you write a message, check any rules about what is and is not considered acceptable in the forum. Many discussion forums have rules, aside from netiquette, about things such as links to commercial sites.
- Take a little time to use the forum's search facilities to see if your question or topic has already been discussed or covered in a set of frequently asked questions (FAQs). If it has, you should at least scan the existing messages to see if your points have been addressed.
- Don't feel you have to post immediately. Take your time to see what is being discussed and get a feel for the group you're joining. This very sensible behaviour has the unfortunate name of *lurking* but is quite acceptable online. If you want to post, many discussion groups have a forum devoted to new users where they can introduce themselves to other readers. These are always good places to get started.
- Try to keep your messages short and to the point. People don't want to read long, rambling messages, especially if they can't work out what response you're looking for.
- Write a concise subject line (title) for your message – people often won't spend time reading messages unless the subject line looks relevant.
- Keep to one subject (topic of discussion) per message. If you want to cover another subject, do it in another message.
- When replying to a message, quoting part of that earlier message can be helpful so that readers can easily see what you are referring to. Add your response *after* the quoted material, not before it. And keep your quotation short and to the point, otherwise the resulting messages will get longer and longer.
- If you ask a question and it is answered, thank the person who responded. It's not only polite, it also shows that the discussion has come to an end.
- If you've reached a point where you disagree with someone and neither of you is going to change your opinion (Figure 8), realise the conversation is over, agree to disagree, and move on.

Activity 10 (exploratory)

In the resources page associated with this part on the TU100 website, you will find a link to a quiz on netiquette. When convenient, go online and use this quiz to test your understanding of what you have studied so far in this session. Then go on to the next activity, which also requires you to be online.

Figure 8 Online discussions can become addictive!

Activity 11 (exploratory)

This module is called *My digital life*, and so far in this part I have explained a little about what a digital life might include. Now it's time for you to tell other people a bit about yourself. You are a member of a tutor group that consists of several other students and your tutor. You may not have had the chance for a face-to-face meeting, so this is your opportunity to introduce yourself.

Post a short message to your tutor-group forum, introducing yourself to your fellow students and your tutor. If your tutor-group forum is not yet open, you can prepare your posting in advance.

There are no hard and fast rules about what to say – all of us have different feelings about what we like to share with others. Some of us will say anything to anyone, some of us are more reticent. Only say what you're comfortable with. Don't worry if you're feeling a little shy – you won't be the only one.

A good start might be telling your colleagues your name and your town. Perhaps you'd like to say if you're employed (and if so what your job is), if you've recently left school, if you're at home with children or with caring responsibilities, or retired? Is this your first Open University module? How about your knowledge of computers and information technology? Are you a novice in the field? What do you expect to get out of TU100 and why did you choose it? These are just examples – as long as you follow netiquette, it's up to you!

Break point
This would be a good point to take a break if you need to do something else before returning later.

3.2   Ethical and legal considerations

In using a computer for communications you have many rights of free expression, but you also have certain responsibilities to respect others. You will learn more about digital technologies and the law in a later part, but at this stage you need to have some awareness of privacy and confidentiality in relation to online communications. The main points you should be aware of are as follows.

- An email is generally considered to be equivalent to a private letter, and should not be quoted or forwarded to anyone else without the permission of the original sender. This can be particularly poorly observed in companies (even those whose employees are told to assume that all online communications are for the recipient's eyes only, unless otherwise stated).

- Besides the informal rules of netiquette, most forums have a code of conduct and conditions of use that govern acceptable behaviour. Your use of the online forums provided by The Open University is covered by the OU Computing Code of Conduct, further information about which is provided in the Computing Guide. You will usually find a forum's terms of use linked from its home page, or listed in the code of conduct that you are asked to agree to when you first register for an account.

- Considerations of copyright and *plagiarism* (cheating by using another person's work as if it were your own) apply to online discussions. If you are quoting something written by someone else, put it in quotation marks and acknowledge the source.

- Some forums are not wholly public, in which case messages should not be copied outside the forum. The forum's terms of use may specify this.

3.3   Copyright

One of the reasons the Web has grown so quickly, and one of its most fascinating aspects, is that almost anyone can publish almost anything on it. It is very easy to find information, images, audio and video files on the Web, which you can then save and incorporate into your own material.

Copying is so easy that people often make the mistake of assuming that everything on the Web is freely available. This is not the case: most information you will come across is likely to be covered by copyright law. This applies not only to online television programmes, music, photographs, books and so on, but also to information – for example, in the form of online academic papers or simply in someone's blog.

Material not subject to copyright is said to belong in the *public domain* and can be used by anyone. Older works of art and literature, such as the works of Shakespeare and Beethoven, are in the public domain. However, individual printings, adaptations or recordings of those works are copyrighted to the publisher or performer. The situation can become very complicated because the duration and extent of copyright differs between countries. For example, material may be in the public domain in the USA but still under copyright in the UK. As a result, it is always wise to assume that any third-party material (that is, material originating from someone else) is still protected by copyright unless you're sure it's in the public domain.

Copyright holders can prosecute individuals and organisations for infringing their rights; in recent years, music and film companies have sued individuals for very large sums of money. Below are some general points you should bear in mind.

- You should seek the author's permission if you wish to use any copyrighted material. Just because something is on the Web does not mean it is freely available for you to use.

- Many websites have usage policies explaining how their material can be used. Some are more restrictive than others, so make sure you find and follow the relevant policies.

- Information published online may have been put there by someone who is not the copyright holder.

- When quoting text in your own academic work (other than in assignment answers – see below), the generally accepted guideline from copyright legislation is that you can use a whole chapter or up to 5% of any one book without seeking permission, but you must give a full reference to show where it has come from.

This may all seem rather intimidating, but it's not quite as bad as you might fear – fortunately, copyright law makes some concessions to students. As a result, you don't have to ask permission to use copyrighted material in answering an assignment question, although you must still include references. However, if you want to reuse the same material for any other purpose at a later date, normal copyright law applies and you must seek permission.

3.4 Good academic practice

One of the things TU100 encourages you to do is use the Web as a resource in your digital life. You'll use it as part of your studies and in your assignments, and you should find it a great help in understanding and practising the things you learn.

However, using information found on the Web in this way can cause problems unless you take a little care. When using material written by other people you can quote their words (as you saw above), but good academic practice is that such quotations should always be *limited* and *acknowledged*. This applies whether you're quoting from the TU100 materials or from other sources such as websites, journals or newspapers.

It can be very tempting to copy and paste large chunks of text into your notes – and possibly then into your assignment answers – without giving a reference. However, that is very bad academic practice. It's far better to use quotations sparingly and to rewrite most of the material in your own words. This allows you to show that you've understood the material and it also helps you to remember it.

In addition, it's good academic practice to give a reference to the source of any third-party material you include in your own work. Not doing so is not only impolite, as you're failing to acknowledge the help that someone else's work has given you; it's regarded as plagiarism and is never acceptable.

TU100 will teach you the correct way to use the work of others and help you to establish good academic habits. As well as using information found on the Web, you will be asked to collaborate with other students to create and share information. You'll also be encouraged to discuss aspects of the module in your tutor-group forum. Both of these activities will help you to develop academic practices that will stand you in good stead in future studies, as well as being valuable skills more generally. You can probably guess that, just as with other third-party materials you make use of, it's important to give references to the contributions of other students when you include them in your own work; otherwise you could fall into the trap of plagiarising their work, which is definitely something to be avoided.

Unless you are specifically asked to do so in the TU100 materials, you should not pass your work on to other students, especially if it is part of an assignment. One good reason for this is that The Open University uses detection software that is very good at spotting plagiarism in assignments! If you're in any doubt about what is acceptable and what is not then do ask your tutor. The boundary between collaboration and plagiarism is sometimes not clear, and your tutor will help you understand whether you are in danger of crossing it.

To help you with this, the OU Library's website provides a guide on how to reference sources of information correctly, including those you might find online. Links to that and to several other useful sites on how to follow good academic practice and avoid plagiarism are in the resources page associated with this part on the TU100 website. It's very important that you follow those links and work through the material when you can, so please make time to do so when you've completed this part.

3.5   Conclusion

In this session I've discussed some of the ways in which you can make good use of the Web, both for interacting with other people and for finding information. When working online it is also important to consider how to protect yourself and your computer, and that's what I'll turn to next.

Online safety

4

The internet provides many ways for people to get in touch with each other, but this ease of contact can have downsides for the unwary. It can expose internet users to the dangers of malicious software, to unsolicited and nuisance emails, and to a variety of hoaxes. In this session I'll describe some of these problems and suggest how you can protect yourself from them.

4.1 Malware

Software designed to cause damage is known as *malware*. There are several types of malware, three of which are described below. However, be aware that as malware evolves to avoid detection, the boundaries between the different categories are tending to blur.

The best-known type of malware is probably the *virus*. This is a piece of software that has been written to attack software on your computer, often with the specific intention of causing harm – deleting files, for example. A virus attaches itself to other software on your computer and activates when that software is run. Viruses are so called because they are designed to spread quickly and easily from one computer to another via internet connections or external storage devices such as memory sticks.

Another type of malware is the *worm*. This is a piece of malicious software that runs 'in the background', doing some damage to your computer even though you may not realise it is running. Worms can make copies of themselves, and those copies can spread via an internet connection. A worm typically consumes resources by running on a computer; in a major attack, all of a computer's processing resources could be used in running the worm and its copies.

Finally, the *trojan* is a digital equivalent of the legendary wooden horse that smuggled Greek soldiers into Troy. It appears to be legitimate software, such as a screensaver, but behind the scenes it is causing damage – perhaps allowing someone else to gain control of the computer, copying personal information, deleting information, or using email software to pass itself on to other computers.

Timings
This is the fourth study session in Part 1. It should take you around two hours to complete. If you don't have time to work through it all at once, there are break points where you can stop and return later.

Protecting your computer

There are three main ways to protect your computer against malware.

- Ensure that your computer has the latest *patch* from the producer of your *operating system (OS)*. Microsoft, Apple and other producers frequently issue patches for their products.

- Make sure other software is kept up to date – Adobe Reader, Flash, Java and web browsers (such as Internet Explorer, Opera, Firefox, etc.) to name just a few. As new malware is discovered, so new versions of software are released that guard against it.

- Install *anti-virus software* and keep it up to date. Anti-virus software catches a very high percentage of malware, but only if the version on your computer is regularly updated. Remember that if you don't use Windows, it is still possible to pass on files infected with malware to Windows users. That's why the main job of anti-virus software for Apple's OS X is to check files for things that could infect Windows machines.

In addition, you can use a piece of software called a *firewall*. This tries to stop unauthorised access to your computer without impeding your own authorised online access. There may be a firewall built into your computer's operating system; others may be present in the hardware that connects your computer to the internet.

As well as the technical protections described above, you should protect yourself by using anti-virus software to scan any files you receive before you open them. This should include:

- files you download from the Web
- files given to you on removable media such as a CD or memory stick
- files attached to emails.

Bear in mind that no reputable software company sends unsolicited email messages with attachments, claiming to be giving you an update.

4.2 Spam

Spam is the general term for unsolicited emails sent to large numbers of people. Such emails could be hoax messages designed to mislead, or they could be used to advertise a product.

In terms of advertising, spam email is similar to the marketing leaflets and letters that drop through your letterbox at home. However, this paper mail is subject to legislation that tightly controls the range of products and services being offered. The equivalent legislation does not yet exist in the electronic world, although new laws are being introduced. For example, in the USA the federal law 'Controlling the Assault of Non-Solicited Pornography and Marketing' (CAN-SPAM) took effect in January 2004, whilst in Europe the EU 'Directive on Privacy and Electronic

Communications' came into force in the latter part of 2003. Though such national legislation is intended to limit the volume of spam email, in practice this is a very difficult task because the internet crosses national borders. Spam can be sent from one country to another, and countries that have legislation find it hard to enforce their rules in countries that do not.

Spam email can be sent only if the *spammer* (the person initiating the spam) has a collection of email addresses to send to. Common ways to 'harvest' email addresses include:

- company databases
- websites
- online discussion groups
- including links in images within emails, which when clicked by the recipient inform the spammer that the message has been opened
- infecting unprotected computers with malicious software to look for addresses.

Spammers may harvest vast numbers of email addresses, but not immediately know whether a particular email address is 'live' (actually in use) – it could be that the original owner of the address no longer uses it. So beware of spam emails that appear to give you the option to unsubscribe from a mailing list (very often by offering a web link to click on). If you select this option, this will verify to the spammers that your email address is live; they can then continue to send you spam, or even sell your email address to other spammers. So using the unsubscribe option can increase your spam rather than reduce it.

Below are some guidelines for minimising the spam you receive.

- Don't reply to spam emails.
- Don't use the unsubscribe option in response to unrequested emails.
- Don't reveal your email address unless you want to receive mail from a particular source.
- Don't post your email address on a website.
- Don't use your regular email address when registering on websites or joining discussion groups. Either create a new email address for these purposes or use a spare one that you're happy to abandon if necessary (e.g. a web-based email account such as those offered by Yahoo, Microsoft, Google, etc.).
- Set your email software to filter out unwanted messages. Most email software is equipped with 'junk mail' filters that can be set to identify and remove spam messages as they arrive in your inbox. Additionally, your *internet service provider (ISP)* may filter incoming mail for spam before it even reaches your inbox.
- Ensure that all other users of your computer follow the above guidance.

Break point
This would be a good point to take a break if you need to do something else before returning later.

4.3   Hoaxes

A hoax message aims to mislead, often relying on the naivety of its recipients. One of the most notorious hoaxes concerned the so-called 'Good Times virus'. This hoax is described by Sophos (n.d.), a company that develops anti-virus software, as follows.

> Probably the most successful virus hoax of all time, Good Times has been scaring people since 1994. It's still going strong, despite the fact that it is completely untrue; there is no such virus, and indeed it is impossible for a virus to do what is claimed for Good Times.

> The hoax started off simply: it warned people not to read or download any email with the subject of "Good Times", because the messages were viral and would erase their hard drives. Later, more detail was added, telling of the damage that would be done to the user's computer system.

> The end of the spoof warning contained an exhortation to "Forward this to all your friends. It may help them a lot." […] In their thousands, people did, and still do.

> The secret to the success of the hoax is that it successfully taps into computer users' fears about computers, security and the Internet, and contains pseudo-technical babble that sounds convincing.

Remember this is a hoax, so please don't spread the news about the Good Times virus as so many others did!

This description indicates how convincing the message in this case was. Hoax messages can spread rapidly via email and forums, often passed on unwittingly by work colleagues, family, friends and even reputable online retailers. Unfortunately, users who fall for hoaxes can cause problems both for themselves and for others. A hoax can generate spam (when, as with Good Times, it directs the recipient to pass on the message), cause files to be deleted unnecessarily and potentially harmfully (by directing the user to delete them), and generally cause panic.

Like Sophos, most anti-virus software vendors maintain information on hoaxes on their websites, so you can check such sites if you suspect a hoax. Alternatively you can use a search engine: by searching for significant terms contained within the hoax message, you may find reports on reputable sites such as the Sophos site.

4.4   Phishing

A particular kind of hoax message aims to persuade users to disclose private information such as credit card details and PIN. This is described as *phishing*. The recipient of the message may be directed to a hoax website where they are requested to part with their details. Figure 9 shows an example of an email that I received.

Figure 9   An attempt at phishing

Activity 12 (exploratory)

Looking at the email in Figure 9, what warning signs are there that might alert you to the fact that this is an attempt at phishing?

Comment

Below are the warning signs I noted when I received this email.

- Although the sender's email address is described as 'HSBC Bank PLC', the actual address – pontiusfamily@netzero.net – appears to have nothing whatsoever to do with the bank; instead it sounds like a private email address.

- The email address of 'netzero.net' refers to an internet service provider – NetZero – based in the USA. I can't imagine that a bank based in the UK would contact me from an email address supplied by an internet service provider in another country.

- There is confusion about which bank this email is meant to be from, as the message refers to both HSBC and Barclays.

- The message exhibits poor grammar and spelling – 'proctect', for example. I think it unlikely that such errors would be present in genuine messages from my bank.
- The message is not addressed to the recipient (me) by name. This can indicate a message sent randomly to large numbers of email addresses.

The above points, along with the fact that I don't actually manage my bank account online, convinced me not to follow the instructions in the message. Yet despite all these warning signs, some people do hand over their details in this way.

It's very important not to click on any links in these sorts of messages. Even if you don't enter your account details, making any response at all may confirm to the phisher that your email address is valid, leaving you open to further hoaxes and spam. Simply clicking on a link also risks your computer being infected with malware that could distribute the same message to all the email addresses – including those of your work colleagues, family and friends – stored on your computer.

One way to check this kind of message is to position your mouse pointer over the link ('Click here' in the Figure 9 example) and look at the web address that appears either as pop-up text or at the bottom of the message window. If it seems to be unrelated to the sender of the message then you should be even more suspicious. After receiving the email shown in Figure 9, I searched online and found a reputable site (millersmiles.co.uk) that contained the information shown in Figure 10.

Most phishing messages try to get you to provide some personal information (Figure 11). Clearly those trying to get your online banking details are aiming to get access to your money. However, others could be trying to access your email, blog, instant messaging or online auction accounts (if you have any), then use these accounts to distribute more phishing emails.

IT stands for *information technology*. This term is often used to mean the same as ICT.

If you have a job that provides you with an email account then you have probably also seen messages claiming to be from your company's IT department, asking you to enter your username and password into a website to reset your email account. I've certainly had them sent to my Open University email account. As with requests for you to disclose your financial details, you should be careful when disclosing your username and password. A phone call to the relevant people in the company should be sufficient to find out whether or not the request is genuine.

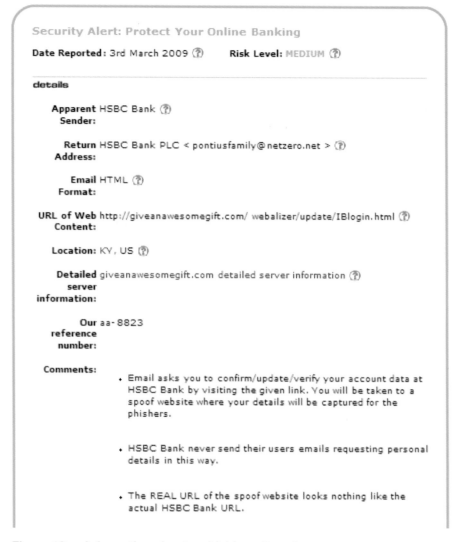

Figure 10   Information about a phishing attempt

Figure 11   Phishing: fooling someone into giving away secret information

Break point
This would be a good point to take a break if you need to do something else before returning later.

4.5 Managing your identity online

As we live more of our lives online, so it becomes more important for us to be aware of and, as far as possible, try to manage the information that others can access about us online. You'll learn more about this in a later part but, as a general guideline, before you place any kind of information about yourself on the Web you should think about the impression you would like potential employers, new friends, your parents or your children to get of you if they searched for you online. Stories of people being disciplined or even losing their jobs as a result of inappropriate comments or photographs on their blogs or social networking sites show that this isn't a hypothetical situation. For some employers, checking the information that is available online about job applicants is as much a part of the selection process as taking up references.

Activity 13 (exploratory)

Enter your name into a search engine and review what you find.

(a) What is revealed about you?

(b) What is revealed about other people with the same name as you? If you have a common name then it may be hard to tell the difference between you and others with the same name. However, you should be able to get an impression – and possibly even some photographs – of a few individuals who share your name. If you can't find anyone with your name, try looking for the name of a family member or friend. Make some notes on one or more of the people you find and post them to your tutor-group forum.

Comment

(a) My name (John Woodthorpe) isn't very common, so most of the links I found do refer to me. They include articles and papers I wrote both before and after I started working for The Open University, as well as links to the OU website and some defunct ones to a website I used to run and took down many years ago. I didn't find my Facebook page because the privacy settings mean that it isn't publicly available.

(b) There were several references to a company director who shares my name. I also found a couple of Facebook users, including one in New Zealand. Most surprisingly, I found a reference to a couple whose names are the same as mine and my wife's – as far as I can tell, they run (or perhaps ran) a guest house in Bulgaria. In addition, there were several links to genealogy sites where people are trying to trace their family trees, and quite a few references to people called John from places called Woodthorpe.

This so-called 'ego surfing' or 'vanity surfing' is an interesting thing to do from time to time. Overall I haven't found anything unpleasant or embarrassing, but I'm old enough for any youthful indiscretions to have happened long before they could have been recorded online. I also have a range of usernames that don't resemble my real name and so aren't easily connected to me. They aren't used for anything nefarious, but I see no reason why I should make it easy for others to find out everything about me.

Several online communities offer good advice on managing your online identity, and you'll find some links to relevant material in the resources page associated with this part on the TU100 website. It's not something to get overly worried about, but it is worth being aware of the impression that others can get by following the trail of your online activities.

4.6 Conclusion

In this session I've discussed ways in which you can protect your computer and yourself online, ranging from taking sensible precautions against malware to guarding against presenting information about yourself to the world that you might later regret.

Summary

In this part I've introduced several aspects of our increasingly digital lives that you will be learning more about, and indeed experiencing yourself, during your study of TU100. You've heard about the ever more significant role that digital technologies are playing in our information society, in areas ranging from entertainment to public services. Along with the opportunities available in the online world, you've also been introduced to some of the potential problems and how to avoid them.

In Part 2 of this block you'll learn more about the development of the computer. Before you move on to that, however, it is important that you take stock of what you've learned so far. As explained in the *TU100 Guide*, learning outcomes express what it is expected you will learn, so considering them at the end of each part is a good way to check your progress.

Activity 14 (self-assessment)

As for all the parts in this block, you should now complete the learning outcomes activity described in the *TU100 Guide*. You'll find an electronic version of the activity table used there in the 'Study resources' section on the left-hand side of the TU100 website. Download and complete that document for Block 1 Part 1, following the instructions in the *TU100 Guide* (which are repeated in the downloadable file).

Apart from the partially completed example in the *TU100 Guide*, no answer is provided for this activity as your response will be unique to your background and experience of TU100 so far.

If you didn't get a chance to do the 'How digital is your life?' quiz earlier then please do it as soon as you can. You should also ensure that you have investigated the links related to Block 1 Part 1 that are provided on the TU100 website. Otherwise, you're ready to start Part 2, which directly follows this part in the book.

Answers to self-assessment activities

Activity 4

The increase in the number of messages was:

7.7 billion – 6.5 billion = 1.2 billion

The percentage growth is found by dividing the change (1.2 billion) by the starting number (6.5 billion) and multiplying the answer by 100%. This gives:

growth = 1.2/6.5 × 100% = 18.5% in seven months

Glossary

anti-virus software   Software that is specifically written to identify and tackle known viruses.

automated teller machine (ATM)   A machine that allows bank customers to perform certain transactions, such as withdrawing cash from their bank account. Also known as a *cash machine* or *cashpoint*.

biometric   A term that refers to the identification of people using biological characteristics such as fingerprints, iris recognition and DNA analysis.

cable   A set of wires or optical fibres assembled, with a protective coating, for use as a communication medium.

copyright   A legal protection that guarantees that creators of content are rewarded for their work and protects the rights of users.

database   A set of computer-based data that has been organised so that it can be read, written, updated and searched. An example might be a library catalogue.

digital rights management (DRM)   A range of technologies used by copyright owners to control how the content they produce is used.

digital technology   Any technology that is based on representing data as sequences of numbers, i.e. as digital data.

emoticons   Text characters or images that indicate someone's mood by representing a simple facial expression. Text-based emoticons such as :-) are usually intended to be 'read' by tilting your head to one side. Also known as *smileys*.

firewall   A software or hardware filter on a network. In its simplest form, a firewall looks at incoming or outgoing data and decides whether to block it.

forum   An area on the internet designed for discussion, usually on a specific topic. Also known as a *bulletin board system (BBS)*.

global positioning system (GPS)   A set of satellites that continuously transmit their position so that anyone with a suitable receiver can obtain very accurate positioning information.

hardware   The physical components of a computer system. These include the large components such as the screen, the small component parts such as circuit boards, and all the connecting cables.

information and communication technology (ICT)   Technology used in the conveying, manipulation and storage of data by electronic means.

information society   A term used to describe the social and economic changes related to the development and widespread use of information technologies.

instant messaging   Text-based communication between people who are online at the same time.

internet   The global internetwork that has grown from a US government-funded project started in the 1960s.

internet service provider (ISP)   A commercial organisation that provides access to the internet for both individuals and organisations.

malware   Malicious software designed to enter computer systems without the knowledge of the owner. Includes viruses, trojans and worms.

modem   A box of electronics placed between a computer and a telephone line to convert the digital signals from the computer into a form that can be sent by telephone.

moderator   A forum user who has responsibility for managing the forum and 'moderating' discussions to ensure they follow the forum rules.

netiquette   A set of guidelines for online behaviour.

network   A collection of devices that can communicate with each other. Networks vary in size and complexity, connecting anything from a few devices to many millions.

network society   A term that is sometimes used interchangeably with 'information society', but which emphasises how the flow of information depends on networks.

online discussion group   A group of people, often with common interests or aims, communicating over the internet.

operating system (OS)   A collection of programs that manages a computer's resources, provides an interface between the user and the computer, and organises the running of other programs. Examples include Windows, Mac OS and Linux.

patch   A temporary fix to a bug or security problem in a particular piece of software (such as a web browser or an operating system). A patch modifies existing software rather than replacing it with a new version.

phishing   The act of sending a hoax email message that aims to persuade users to disclose private information such as credit card details or pin numbers. Hoax websites are also used as part of these scams.

plagiarism   Using the work of others to gain some form of benefit without formally acknowledging that the work came from someone else.

portal   A website that provides a way in to a number of sites grouped together by organisation, topic, geography, etc.

program   A step-by-step set of precise instructions for telling a computer how to carry out a particular task.

public domain   A term referring to any created content that is not subject to copyright. Material that is 'in the public domain' may be used freely by anyone.

smart device   An electronic device that processes information and exchanges it with other devices.

SMS   The 'short message system' that allows text messages to be sent between mobile phones. SMS messages can also be sent between other devices, such as computers and landline phones.

social networking   The activities involved in building and maintaining online relationships and communities.

software   The programs that control the functioning of a computer system.

spam   Unsolicited (junk) email. Spammers typically send an email to a distribution list consisting of millions of 'harvested' email addresses.

trojan   Malicious software that is disguised as a legitimate program, but that in the background is running some malicious code.

ubiquitous   A term describing something that seems to be everywhere at the same time.

virus   Malicious software that is designed to attack software on users' computers, spreading quickly and easily from one computer to another.

World Wide Web   An internet service that links computer files such as documents, images, audio and video. These files may be located on any computer connected to the internet. Also known as the *Web*.

worm   Malicious software that replicates itself and infects computers via a network.

References

International Telecommunication Union (2006) *ITU Internet Report 2006: digital.life* [online], Geneva, Switzerland, ITU, http://www.itu.int/osg/spu/publications/digitalife/ (accessed 10 January 2010).

Sophos (n.d.) *Good Times* [online], Sophos Plc, http://www.sophos.com/security/hoaxes/goodtimes.html (accessed 12 January 2010).

Text.it (2008) *The Q2 2008 UK Mobile Trends Report* [online], Mobile Data Association, http://www.text.it/mediacentre/press_release_list.cfm?thePublicationID=6F5A90F5-15C5-F4C0-992D5F8DDAF2BDCA (accessed 1 January 2010).

Acknowledgements

Grateful acknowledgement is made to the following sources.

Text
Quotation p. 44: © Sophos Plc

Figures
Figure 1: © Jason Stitt/iStockphoto

Figure 2: © Michigan State University

Figure 3: © Jim Zuckerman/Alamy Images

Figure 4: Courtesy of http://xkcd.com/281/

Figure 5: Courtesy of http://xkcd.com/256/

Figure 6: © Marty Bucella/Cartoon Stock

Figure 8: Courtesy of http://xkcd.com/386/

Figure 10: © www.millersmiles.co.uk/report/8823

Figure 11: Courtesy of http://xkcd.com/565/

Part 2

Anything, anywhere

Author: Tony Nixon

Introduction

The first computers weighed several tonnes, occupied entire buildings and were very rare indeed – in the early 1950s there were fewer than one hundred of them in the world. The notion of portability – simply being able to carry a computer from place to place – as well as the vast range of current uses to which computers are put would have seemed very strange to the people who built and worked with those early machines. Yet today, as you saw in Block 1 Part 1, computers and information technologies are practically everywhere in the world around us, and the processing power of an entire 1950s computer can be found on a *silicon chip* that is hardly visible. In fact, the number of silicon chips in the world is now many times the number of humans!

You will learn more about silicon chips in Session 2.

In this part of TU100 I will relate some of the history of computing, from its very early days to the present. In looking at this I hope you will see that as the role of computers has changed, so our perceptions of what a computer is and how it should be used have altered too. As part of this discussion I will introduce you to modern concepts of computing such as *ubiquity* and the *cloud*, and describe how computers and networks are perceived to be evolving into the future.

I will also show you how aspects of the real world are represented in the digital world. This, in turn, will lead you into learning about binary numbers, the language of computers. Along the way I'll show you a Sense program related to the topics I'm discussing, but at this point all you are expected to do is observe the program in operation, not understand how it works.

I hope this part will help you to see the relationship between our expectations of computers and their evolution, so that you are able confidently to answer questions such as 'What is a computer?' and 'What are (and were) they used for?'.

To start you thinking about the history of computers, I'd like you to share some of your own experience.

Activity 1 (exploratory)

What is the first computer that you remember using? It could be anything from the personal computer (PC) you are using to study TU100 to one you used at work or owned/shared/borrowed in the past. If possible, you should identify the make of the computer, describe it and, if you can, say when you first used it. Can you add anything about your experience – for example, how easy and intuitive to use it was?

Post your responses to this activity to your tutor-group forum. The aim is simply to share this information with other students in your group, and then perhaps to comment on any similarities and differences in your experiences. So, for example, did anyone else encounter the same machines as you? Did they use them for the same activities – work, games, email, etc.? Did they like or dislike working with them? This may form the basis of some interesting discussions, and hopefully it will indicate the range of skills and experiences of the other members of your group.

Comment

The first computer I ever used was a friend's Sinclair ZX81 in about 1980. The ZX81 looked like a flat box about 200 mm square with a keyboard embedded into its upper face. It didn't have a screen, so you had to plug it into the television set, and if you wanted to save a program you needed a cassette recorder – altogether very cumbersome, although the ZX81 itself was quite compact.

As for the experience, at the time it seemed relatively easy to do simple arithmetic on the ZX81, but anything related to *graphics* was fairly tortuous and it was virtually impossible to use without the manual. It also had next to no *memory*, so it was a challenge to do anything substantial.

With your own experiences and those of your fellow students in mind, you are now ready to begin studying this part. Don't forget to update your learning journal after each study session or at the end of the part.

Learning outcomes

Your study of this part will help you to do the following.

Knowledge and understanding

- List some milestones in the history of computing, including that of the personal computer.
- Describe some of the characteristics of the four generations of computers.
- Explain the concepts of ubiquitous computing and cloud computing, and identify their ethical dimensions.
- Identify potential devices in which computers might be embedded.
- Describe how the physical world can be represented in digital form.
- Explain the concept of a number base.
- Describe how binary numbers are stored in a computer.
- Explain the concept of exponential growth.

Cognitive skills

- Convert between decimal numbers and binary numbers.
- Contrast analogue and digital quantities and representations.

Key skills

- Take notes as an aid to learning.
- Read actively as an aid to learning.
- Perform simple calculations related to energy consumption.
- Perform simple calculations relating to computer memory.
- Work with number bases.
- Work with exponential notation in simple contexts, and with prefixes for large numbers such as kilo, mega and giga.
- Keep a learning journal.

Practical and professional skills

- Run a simple Sense program.

Note taking

1

Before I get started on the history of computing, in this brief initial session I want to give you some guidance on note taking for academic learning. This should stand you in good stead for the remainder of this part, and indeed the rest of your studies: you should find that developing your note-taking skills will help you to understand and remember key ideas.

Timings
This session should take you around half an hour to complete.

1.1   Why take notes?

Note taking is a useful skill for academic learning, as it enables you to remember the main points of an article or paper without having to read it all again. The process of summarising helps you to make connections and reflect on what you have read. While you are studying you will usually be taking notes for your own use, but in fact note taking is a generally useful skill to develop as it can be used at work or in other activities.

Later parts will discuss different forms of note taking, to help you develop your skills further.

1.2   Guidance on note taking

When taking notes the first thing you have to consider is what they are going to be used for, since notes taken for one purpose may not be suitable for another. Here are some possibilities:

- to help you understand the information
- to help you remember the information
- to help you explain the information to someone else
- to highlight the points that will be useful in an assignment
- to help you revise
- to reveal the underlying structure and arguments of the text.

When writing notes, you should bear in mind the following points.

- They should be personal – the notes are usually for your benefit, so they won't look like anyone else's notes. Use whatever language helps you relate to and understand the information.
- They should have a purpose, or perhaps several purposes as outlined above. When writing your notes you should be clear as to what their purpose is, and keep this in mind as you write them. If you feel you

are drifting from your purpose then you may need to make adjustments.

- They should be the length you want – don't feel you have to be either more concise or more detailed. The notes should fit whatever their purpose is for you. You may wish to make more detailed notes about one section and less detailed notes about another, depending on your need.

- They should make sense later – there is often a temptation to jot down single words that you understand perfectly at the time but that may not mean anything to you a few months later.

- They should be readily available – you could make notes using Word or other word-processing software, or you may prefer to make notes on paper or in your personal blog.

1.3   When is the right time to take notes?

Any time that suits you! We live in an age where increasingly there is more information available to us than we can possibly hope to deal with. One of the most important skills that you (or any of us) can develop is the ability to cope with all this information. Note taking is just one technique that will help you to do this. It is important to get into the habit of making notes, and the best way to do this is to find a method that suits you (and the medium you are working in).

1.4   How to take notes

So what should you do when taking notes? Again you will develop your own technique, but the method I use is as follows: I read the material once very quickly from start to finish, then sift back through it noting down the words or phrases I think are important. I usually do this in a word processor, but you can just as easily use pen and paper. Avoid simply copying and pasting large chunks of material; it is the process of actively reading the material and putting it into your own words that makes note taking useful. Merely copying and pasting defeats the object, although you may decide to paste in short quotations.

1.5   Alternative ways to take notes

Some people prefer to take notes in a non-linear way and to be able to visualise the connections between different ideas. You may have heard of one or more of the following: *spray diagrams*, *mind maps*, *spider diagrams* and *concept maps*. These are all ways in which you can present ideas or information in a diagram rather than as text. They are essentially the same in terms of their structure, but are used for different functions. *Mind maps* and *concept maps* are used when developing your own ideas on a subject, for example when planning a report or essay. *Spray diagrams* and

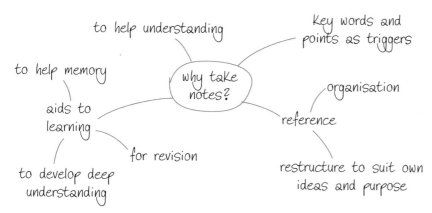

Figure 1   Spray diagram (adapted from Giles and Hedge, 1994, p. 212)

spider diagrams summarise ideas that other people have written or spoken – in other words, they are ideal for note taking. I will concentrate on spray diagrams.

Figure 1 shows an example of a spray diagram about note taking. The core topic is shown in the circle in the centre of the diagram. Main themes are linked by lines from the central circle. Some of these themes then have sub-themes that branch outwards. The points further from the centre are usually more detailed and specific than the central topics.

1.6   Extra help

If you are new to studying or haven't done this kind of thing for a long time, you may want more practice at reading and note taking than is provided here. If so, the resources page associated with this part on the TU100 website provides some additional materials that have been developed for use by OU students, which you may find helpful. These are not specific to TU100, so some of the examples might be unfamiliar to you, but they have intentionally been developed to suit OU students of any subject area.

Activity 2 (exploratory)

You are about to study Session 2, which focuses on the history of computing. Treat your study of this session as an opportunity to try using spray diagrams for note taking. Obviously these won't fit in the margins of the printed text, so you'll have to use a separate piece of paper – maybe several pieces. Remember, you are taking notes in order to help you engage with the text.

Once you reach the end of the subsection 'The ENIAC', I will show you what my own spray diagram looks like at that point.

1.7 Conclusion

To start your studies off on the right foot, in this session I have discussed note taking and how to approach it. You will continue to develop your skills in this area throughout TU100.

This session should have helped you with the following learning outcomes.

- Take notes as an aid to learning.
- Read actively as an aid to learning.

Computers, but not as we know them

2

I'm now going to take you on a short tour of the history of computing, identifying some of the trends that have emerged and highlighting a few of the more significant stages and developments in technology that have led us to where we are today. As part of this you will watch a video. Don't forget to try your hand at using spray diagrams.

At this stage you may be wondering why you need to know anything about the historical development of computing. After all, to make a journey you only have to know where you're going, not where you've been. The answer to this is that where computers are concerned there is no obvious destination, because the technologies involved are – and always have been – in a state of rapid development. This continual development is due not only to our ability to create new technologies to address particular challenges, but also to our creativity and vision in applying emerging technologies in new ways. Studying a little of the history will enable you to stand back and take a more objective view, to see the paths of development and application and how they influence each other. It should also give you some idea of the incredible rate of development that has taken place over the last few decades, which in turn will give you a feel for some of the developments that may still be in store.

This session is not intended to be a definitive history of the computer; such a history would run to several volumes. However, after studying this session you should be able to identify a few of the milestones in the development of computers and particularly in the development of the personal computer (PC) – although, as you will learn later, personal computers are far from being the most common form of computing device.

There is a general acceptance that, to date, four generations of computer can be identified. Although this isn't universally agreed, it is very convenient to be able to group computers in this way when describing their development, and so I will now look at each of the generations in turn.

Timings
This session should take you around two hours to complete, but you don't have to work through it all at once.

2.1 The first generation

Computing has its origins in mechanical devices that were designed to help solve arithmetical problems. There are many working examples and designs stretching back over the last few hundred years – several thousand years, if you include such things as the Greek Antikythera clockwork mechanism (Figure 2) and the abacus.

The answer to the question of which of these was the first computer largely depends on how you choose to define a computer. In TU100 the focus is on *programmable electronic computers*, which first emerged around the time of the Second World War (1939–1945 AD).

Programmable computers

What do I mean by programmable? You can think of a program as a set of instructions, such as:

- add two numbers
- then divide the result by three.

The result will vary depending on which two numbers I input to the program, which is useful. For example, if I input the numbers 5 and 7 then the result given by the program is 4; if I input 15 and 6 then the output is 7. More significantly, I can change the set of instructions to do something different, such as:

- subtract one value from the other
- then multiply the result by four.

Figure 2   The Antikythera mechanism, part of an astronomical clock built *c.*150–100 BC

This implies a level of versatility, since I can change the set of instructions (the program) in order to produce different results. It's this ability to change the instructions that makes a machine programmable.

> As well as the term *program* when talking about computers, you will also encounter the term *data*. In the examples above, the data are the numbers entered and those output by the program. The word *data* is actually plural (*datum* refers to an item of data) but is often used in the singular, e.g. 'The data is …'. You will find both uses in TU100, depending on the context.

Electronics

At the heart of every modern computer are *electronic switches*. Box 1 explains more about electricity and its associated terminology, but here all you really need to know is that each switch can be either on or off. These states, on and off, can be thought of as representing the digits 1 and 0: when a particular switch is on it represents the digit 1, when off it represents the digit 0. Multiple switches can be set to different combinations of on/off to represent different sequences of 0s and 1s. You will see later in this part that every number can be represented by a unique sequence of this kind; such a sequence is known as a *binary number*. For example, the number 23 is equivalent to the binary number 10111. I don't expect you to understand any of the details of this yet, but you should be able to imagine how a set of switches, each one either on or off, can represent ordinary numbers using their binary equivalents. For example, 23 could be represented using five switches: the first one on, the second one off and the final three on.

This ability to represent numbers using switches forms the basis of the programming capabilities of computers. The key to making a good computer is the ability to make switches that can be operated quickly and reliably with a minimum of effort.

Box 1 Electrical terminology

Because we are dealing with electronic computers, from time to time you will encounter terms such as *current*, *voltage* and *power*. At this stage you might find it useful to have a feel for what these terms mean in relation to electricity. Be assured, though, that you are not expected to understand the finer points of electrical theories!

The easiest way to visualise electricity is as a flow of fundamental particles we call *electrons*. By pushing electrons through various materials we can get them to do work for us. We call this flow of electrons the *current*. Just like the current of water in a river, the stronger the flow of electrons the more current we have. In a river, the strength of flow depends on the slope that the river flows down: the steeper the slope, the stronger the flow. With electricity, the current is produced by the strength of an electric force field. The push of this field on the electrons is called the *voltage* and is measured in *volts*; the current is measured in *amperes*.

In brief:

- The current is a measure of the flow of electrons. We measure this in *amperes*, usually abbreviated to *amps* or simply A.

- The voltage is a measure of how hard the electrons are pushed. This is measured in *volts* and given the symbol V.

Finally, I need to say something about *power*. Imagine a water wheel being pushed around by a river. I can use this wheel to drive (or power) machinery. If the machinery is heavy I will need either a lot of water pushing my wheel or a very fast flow (Figure 3). So it is with electricity; the more powerful the device or machine that is driven by electricity, the higher the current or the voltage required. The *power* provided by the voltage and current, which is measured in *watts*, is found by multiplying the voltage by the current.

Incidentally, as you will see when I discuss power consumption shortly, power is often more conveniently measured in kilowatts where

1 kilowatt = 1000 watts

or even megawatts where

1 megawatt = 1000 000 watts

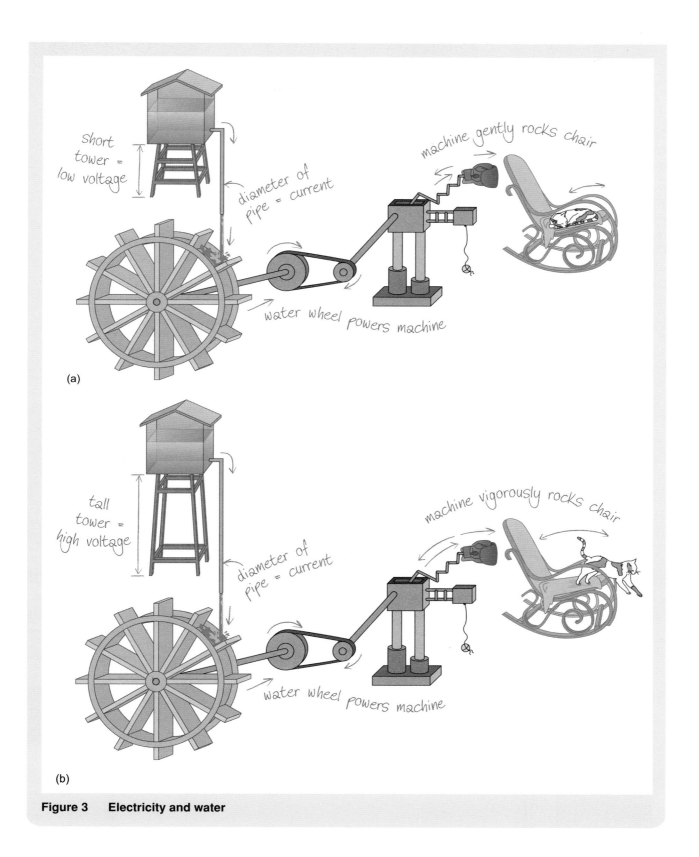

short tower = low voltage

diameter of pipe = current

machine gently rocks chair

water wheel powers machine

(a)

tall tower = high voltage

diameter of pipe = current

machine vigorously rocks chair

water wheel powers machine

(b)

Figure 3   Electricity and water

Colossus

Colossus was the name given to a series of machines created and used at Bletchley Park in England during the Second World War. These machines, which are fine examples of very early programmable electronic computers, were dedicated to breaking codes produced by the German cipher machines known as Lorenz machines. You will learn about using computers to break codes in a later part.

As their name indicates, the Colossus machines were quite large (Figure 4). They used bulky, expensive thermionic valves (see Box 2) as electronic switches. A Colossus machine was fed using paper tape with holes punched in it to represent data. This tape was read into the machine at a speedy 30 mph and the output was to an electric typewriter (effectively a printer).

Such was the secrecy surrounding the work done at Bletchley Park, in particular the deciphering of the Lorenz codes, that information relating to Colossus only entered the public domain in 1970. You will see a replica of a Colossus machine in action and hear it described by its constructor, Tony Sale, when you watch the video at the end of this session.

The Colossus machines are often wrongly associated with cracking the codes generated by the more widely used Enigma machines. The Lorenz machines were used by the German high command and were much less portable than the Enigma machines, which were used in the field.

Figure 4   A Colossus machine at Bletchley Park

Box 2 Thermionic valves

In the 1940s the best candidates for electronic switches were *thermionic valves*, often simply referred to as *valves*. A thermionic valve is a glass vacuum tube that contains a hot wire, a grid and a positively charged terminal called an anode (Figure 5). By varying a small voltage on the grid, it is possible to vary the flow of current between the hot wire and the anode, thus forming an electronic *amplifier*. If the grid voltage is altered quickly enough then the valve acts as a switch.

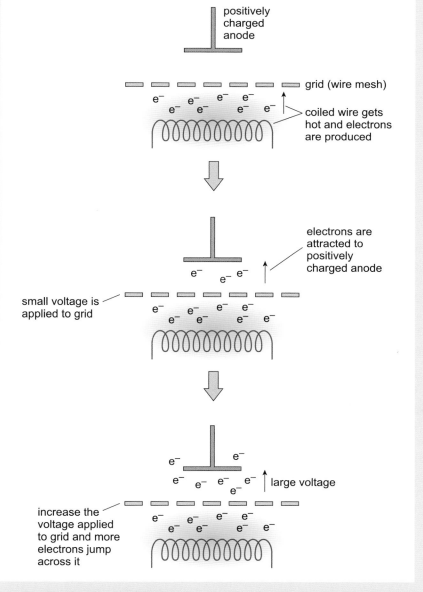

Figure 5   How a valve works

To help you think about amplification, imagine turning on a tap in a washbasin: you apply a small amount of pressure to release the water. In the same way, applying a small voltage to the grid of a valve releases a large current. If you continue to open the tap then you are amplifying (increasing) the flow of water. Similarly, if you increase the voltage on the grid then more current flows across the valve.

Now imagine what might be possible if you could control the tap using water, rather than turning it by hand. You could connect a series of taps together so that the flow of water from each tap controlled one or more taps below it. Of course, to control more than one tap using a single tap, you would need plenty of water. Thus in order to build an effective computer you need amplification as well as switching. Amplification is important because it allows you to use one switch to control the states of many other switches.

There were many disadvantages to valve technology: valves had a limited life expectancy, they were large and they consumed a lot of electrical power. For a computer to be of any use it needed to have thousands or even tens of thousands of valves. Thus the computers of the 1940s were unreliable, heavy and inefficient compared to the machines of today.

The ENIAC

The first *general-purpose* computer (remember that Colossus was a set of highly dedicated machines) was probably the ENIAC (Electronic Numerical Integrator and Computer). This was built at the University of Pennsylvania in the USA, again for military applications and again using valve technology. The ENIAC weighed about 27 tonnes and occupied 63 square metres of floor space (it was 26 metres long); obviously, portability was not a priority! Figure 6 should give you an idea of its size.

Like many of the early computers, the ENIAC was primarily used to process lengthy calculations for the US military, particularly relating to the hydrogen bomb and the computing of artillery tables. It was programmed using plugs and wires, and required a team of operators to set it up and run it. Though it may seem odd to us now that a program was represented in this way, all a program does is establish an electronic circuit in which switches are turned on and off – so why not use plugs and wires to establish the circuit?

Figure 6   The ENIAC

Of course, as you can probably imagine, the ENIAC was cumbersome to use. Simply working out how to set up a program reputedly took weeks, and implementing it once it was set up took further days. Also, there was no way to save a program, so to return to the same calculation at some future date would require all the days of implementation to be repeated. In addition to these problems, the ENIAC was initially very unreliable because of valve failures and was under repair almost as frequently as it was working, although this improved as valves became more reliable.

Activity 3 (exploratory)

I asked you in Activity 2 to draw spray diagrams as a form of note taking in this session. Although note taking is a very individual activity, at this point you may find it helpful to look at Figure 7, which is the spray diagram I created whilst working on the first part of this session. How does it compare with yours?

Comment
Your spray diagram may well have looked very different from mine. I would expect you to have found it useful to note roughly the same points as I did, but you probably grouped them differently. You may even have created more than one spray diagram to represent these ideas.

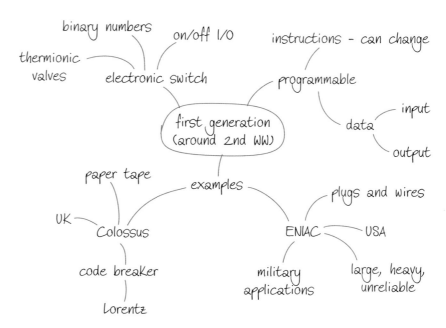

Figure 7   Spray diagram on the first part of Session 2

Storage of instructions

A major step forward came when computer designers realised that they could store instructions in the same way that data was stored: using a number of switches, each set to either on or off. This introduced the possibility of being able to store and recall sets of instructions, rather than wiring them in as was the case with the ENIAC.

By the early 1950s computers were being sold for business use, often for tasks such as payroll calculations and stock control. Although they were still used to carry out calculations, there was a shift towards doing large numbers of simple calculations rather than the lengthy and complex calculations required by the military. For example, a UNIVAC I computer was used to predict the outcome of the 1952 US presidential elections based on statistical analysis of early returns.

UNIVAC stands for Universal Automatic Computer.

Power consumption

At this point it's worth pausing to consider the power consumption of electrical equipment. Power consumption affects different people and organisations in different ways. For some, the potential environmental impacts of power consumption are a key issue; others may be more concerned with the running costs associated with power-hungry items. These are issues that companies such as Google consider very carefully, because they use a vast number of computers.

It's interesting to see how power consumption has altered over time as the technologies have changed. A Colossus machine used about 8 kilowatts, whereas the much larger ENIAC required about 170 kilowatts. Just to give you a feel for the relative power levels involved, Table 1 lists a few familiar devices and their power consumptions.

Table 1 Power consumption of some electrical devices

Device	Power consumption
Electric fire	2 kW
Electric iron	1 kW
46" television	300 W
Desktop computer	300 W
Energy-saving light bulb	10 W
Electric kettle	2 kW

You will notice that in Table 1 I have used an abbreviation for the units of power; instead of kilowatts I write kW and instead of watts I write W. Remember that 1 kW = 1000 W.

In the abbreviation kW, it is worth remembering that the W is upper case and the k lower case.

In order to make a comparison of the power consumptions of these items, you will need to convert all the figures given in kilowatts to watts by multiplying by 1000. For instance, the power consumption of the electric fire is:

$$2 \text{ kW} = 2 \times 1000 \text{ W}$$
$$= 2000 \text{ W}$$

Activity 4 (self-assessment)

(a) Convert the figures given in Table 1 for the electric iron and electric kettle from kilowatts to watts.

(b) Which three devices in the list use the most power?

(c) Can you think of something that these three devices have in common?

Activity 4 shows that generally speaking, heating requires a lot of power. Interestingly, in the case of computers heat is an unwanted by-product – virtually all the power consumed by a computer is converted to heat. The 170 kW converted to heat by the ENIAC would have made it like standing in the room with 85 electric fires running at full power!

Activity 5 (self-assessment)

How did I arrive at the figure of 85 electric fires?

170 kW/85 =
170 kW/2 = 85

Visions of the future

As first-generation computers developed, more people came into contact with them and some began to wonder about the direction in which computers were leading the world. With hindsight, some of the predictions made seem rather pessimistic. Take these two, for example:

> I think there is a world market for maybe five computers.

Attributed to Thomas Watson, Chairman of IBM, 1943

> Where a calculator on the ENIAC is equipped with 18 000 vacuum tubes and weighs 30 tons, computers in the future may have only 1000 vacuum tubes and perhaps weigh 1.5 tons.

Popular Mechanics, March 1949

The 'vacuum tubes' referred to here are the same as the thermionic valves I described in Box 2 above.

On the other hand, others were almost prophetic given the limited technologies of the time. In February 1945 the engineer and popular science-fiction writer Arthur C. Clarke wrote to the magazine *Wireless World* predicting the possibility of communications satellites. This was an astonishing piece of foresight that was totally ignored at the time. In fact, Clarke later stated that when he made this prediction, he thought it might actually prove infeasible because the valves would need changing frequently and the cost of continually sending astronauts into space to do this would be prohibitive. On the basis of computers such as the ENIAC, his reservations are understandable!

Throughout much of the first generation, computers were seen as rather mysterious entities. Some people anticipated that they might develop the potential to think for themselves and even emulate human beings. As early as 1950, the visionary academic Alan Turing proposed that a computer should be deemed 'able to think' if it passed what became known as the *Turing test*. This asks whether a computer can hold a dialogue convincingly enough that the human involved in the conversation is fooled into thinking he or she is talking to another human. As yet, no computer is universally accepted as having passed the Turing test.

Activity 6 (exploratory)

ELIZA is the name of a classic computer program written in the 1960s to demonstrate the power of the computer in a way that could easily be understood by non-computer specialists. It is a very simple interactive program that simulates a conversation between a psychotherapist and a patient – the computer plays the psychotherapist and the user plays the patient!

In experiments, many people who used the program became emotionally involved with ELIZA the 'psychotherapist', even though it was just a computer. In addition, a number of practising psychotherapists who saw the program in action appeared to believe that it could easily be developed into an automated form of psychotherapy.

There is a link to a version of ELIZA in the resources page associated with this part on the TU100 website. When you have a chance, follow this link and try entering some questions or statements. How realistic is the resulting conversation?

Comment

Personally I didn't find that ELIZA did much more than reformulate my own statements. She didn't seem to me to be a very convincing psychotherapist. However, had I not known 'she' was a computer I might have believed that she was human, at least. So perhaps the more interesting question is whether you would have known you were communicating with a computer if you hadn't realised it was a possibility.

2.2   The second generation

The first generation of computers was defined by the use of valve technology and the assumption that the main purpose of computers was to carry out calculations. During the late 1950s, a second generation began to emerge that used *transistors*. A transistor is a tiny crystal of silicon (Figure 8a) that, when processed in various ways, can be made to conduct electrical charges and act as a switch by blocking or allowing electrical current, just like a valve. At only a few millimetres in diameter, a transistor occupied less than a thousandth of the volume of a valve and offered far greater reliability at a fraction of the cost. Additionally, the power consumption of transistors was much lower than that of valves and their switching speed was higher.

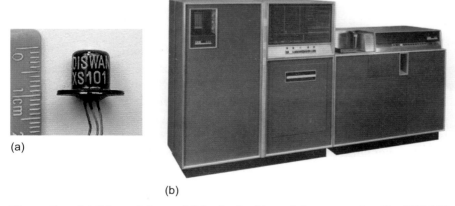

(a)

(b)

Figure 8   (a) A transistor and (b) a typical transistor computer, the IBM 608

However, second-generation computers were still very expensive both to buy and to maintain – for instance, in 1955 IBM's 608 computer (Figure 8b) could be purchased for the bargain price of US$83 000 (or about a quarter of that in pounds), much more than the cost of the average house at the time. They were also far from small; in fact the biggest were referred to as *mainframes*, after the large cabinets that housed them. And although the power consumption of the average computer fell to just a few hundred watts with the emergence of transistor technology, as time went by the complexity of mainframe machines grew and with it their power consumption.

During the early 1960s a new, smaller type of transistor-based computer, usually referred to as a *minicomputer*, entered the market. A minicomputer came in a case about the size of a wardrobe, and had a number of monitors (display screens) and keyboards connected to it. Minicomputers were much cheaper to buy and to run than mainframe computers, costing about US$16 000 in 1964. Although they were still far too expensive and took up far too much space to be suitable for personal ownership, they fell within the reach of smaller businesses. Thus the minicomputer expanded the number of computer users considerably and is often seen as marking the beginning of the third generation.

2.3   The third generation

The third generation was defined by the emergence of the *integrated circuit (IC)* (Figure 9a), otherwise known as the *chip* or *silicon chip*. The first computers that used this technology appeared in 1964. Instead of the individual components (such as transistors) being made from separate crystals of silicon, several components were placed (integrated) on the same crystal. This gave a huge improvement in speed and size, whilst reducing manufacturing costs. Both minicomputers and mainframes moved over to this third-generation technology; Figure 9(b) shows a typical computer from this period.

It was at this point that the way people interacted with computers came close to what we would recognise today. Instead of punched cards for inputting information and paper printouts for output, keyboards began to be used more widely for input and monitors for output, typically with several monitors and keyboards being linked to the same machine. *Terminals*, each of which consisted of a monitor and a keyboard, could be distributed across the country and connected to a single shared computer by telephone lines. These terminals could be used to enter data by filling in forms on screen. This period also saw another significant development in the emergence of the first *floppy disks* for storage, making programs and data truly portable for the first time.

(a)

(b)

Figure 9   (a) A printed circuit board containing about 140 integrated circuits (ICs) and (b) a typical IC-based computer

2.4   The fourth generation

All the computers I have described so far are a long way from today's *personal computers (PCs)*, which trace their origins back to the late 1970s and the emergence of the *microprocessor*, heralding the fourth generation of computers.

A microprocessor is essentially a single integrated circuit that contains the *central processing unit (CPU)* of a computer. The CPU can be thought of as the command centre of the computer; amongst other functions, it interprets each program's instructions and organises the storage and retrieval of the data involved. Third-generation computers had the equivalent of a CPU, of course, but at that time the different components of the CPU were usually distributed across several circuit boards (containing the integrated circuits described earlier) and even across several cabinets or equipment racks.

Developing the CPU into a single component brought considerable benefits, including reduced manufacturing and running costs and the potential to manufacture in very large numbers. There were also benefits in terms of processing speed and, later, being able to eliminate some electronic components altogether. For example, when a key is pressed on a keyboard it is possible for it to seem like a rapid series of presses, because the electrical connection is not always made cleanly; and so early computers required electronic circuits to 'debounce' the keyboard. However, after the development of the microprocessor it became practical to use software to eliminate this stuttering and the circuits previously required to do the 'debouncing' could be removed.

With the introduction of microprocessors, personal ownership of a computer became possible for the first time in history. These early personal computers were often referred to as *microcomputers* or just *micros*.

Activity 7 (self-assessment)

(a) In this session I have described four generations of computer. Identify the technology associated with each generation.

(b) Identify the key benefits commonly involved in moving from one generation to the next.

In my answer to Activity 7 I listed reduction in manufacturing costs as one benefit of the evolution of computers. However, it is important to note that each shift in technology required massive initial investment. The process used for manufacturing microprocessors, for example, has a very high cost associated with the initial design of the components and building the manufacturing equipment, but after this up-front investment the ongoing manufacturing costs are very low. This led to the famous Silicon Valley saying:

The first chip costs a million dollars; the second one costs a nickel.

Silicon Valley is a region of California in the USA that is known for its large number of high-tech industries.

Handwritten margin notes:

(b) each successive generation of computers required less energy for a given task & became faster, smaller and cheaper to use & to manufacture in large #'s

1st Gen – Valves
2nd Gen – Transistors
3rd Gen – Pre-microprocessor Integrated Circuits
4th Gen – Microprocessor

Activity 8 (self-assessment)

The integration of several components into a single component is a common theme in the evolution of computers. The result of this sort of integration is a huge reduction in cost and greatly increased performance, often at a slight cost in flexibility.

(a) Identify two examples of such integration in the descriptions I've given of the four computer generations.

(b) Why might such integration lead to reduced flexibility?

In the late 1970s and early 1980s, a host of popular personal computers emerged that were designed for home use and aimed at mass markets, all based around a narrow range of microprocessors. Typical prices for these machines ranged from about £100 to £500. Many of the companies involved were short-lived; indeed, most never saw the end of the 1980s.

One such computer was the BBC Model B (Figure 10), which cost around £350. This was part of a series of computers known as the BBC Micros, which were built by the Acorn company in a joint enterprise with the BBC – known as the BBC Computer Literacy Project – that aimed to bring computers into schools with accompanying television programmes.

Into the nineties: strands of computing

By the early 1980s several different kinds of computer were emerging, and these continued to develop into the 1990s. There isn't space here for me to

Figure 10   A BBC Model B Micro

describe them all in detail, but in very broad terms you can think of them as making up four strands of evolution, differing in size, cost and purpose. These four strands were as follows:

- Small personal computers, designed primarily for home use and small businesses. Aside from games (which were increasingly attracting people to computers), these were used for *applications* such as word processing, spreadsheets, databases and the like.

- Larger, more expensive *workstations*, which were used for modelling, running sophisticated graphics applications and other similar processor-intensive tasks. These machines were often interconnected in order to share processing power, and so each was a *multi-user computer*, meaning that many users could simultaneously access its resources (CPU or memory, for example).

I introduced you to minicomputers and mainframes during the discussion of the second generation. Those of the 1990s were still quite large multi-user machines, but unlike second-generation machines they were microprocessor based.

- Minicomputers, used for many of the same tasks as workstations. One central minicomputer had distributed terminals, allowing numerous users to interact with the computer. By the early 1990s there was considerable overlap between the roles of workstations and minicomputers. For example, many universities replaced their minicomputers with networks of workstations, to provide email and administrative services alongside their existing role in supporting academic activities such as mathematical modelling.

- The highly expensive mainframes and *supercomputers* used by the defence sector, academics, very large businesses and government organisations. Supercomputers, particularly those made by the Cray Research company (such as the one shown in Figure 11), gained prominence in the 1990s; they were typically used to do complex and numerically intensive work such as modelling weather systems. In the meantime, mainframes were increasingly being used for tasks relating to large databases, such as payroll management.

Figure 11   A supercomputer made by the Cray Research company

Components of a personal computer

The CPU in the form of a microchip remains the key hardware component of computers today. Although more and more elements of the computer have found their way onto the CPU over time, the fundamental layout of most personal computers has remained unchanged since the time of the micro in the late seventies.

Figure 12 shows some of the basic components of a personal computer. You can see that the components 'inside the box' include:

- the CPU
- the *main memory*, sometimes referred to as *random-access memory (RAM)*, which provides temporary storage for data and program instructions whilst a program is running
- the *motherboard*, on which are located the CPU and main memory as well as other key components – the motherboard also provides all the connections for the *peripheral devices*
- the *hard disk drive*, which provides persistent storage for data and programs (i.e. it stores data until you choose to delete it)
- the *CD/DVD drive*, which reads from and writes to CDs/DVDs.

Then there are external peripheral devices, such as:

- the keyboard, printer and monitor, which are connected to the computer by cables.

You will learn more about the components of a personal computer in a later part.

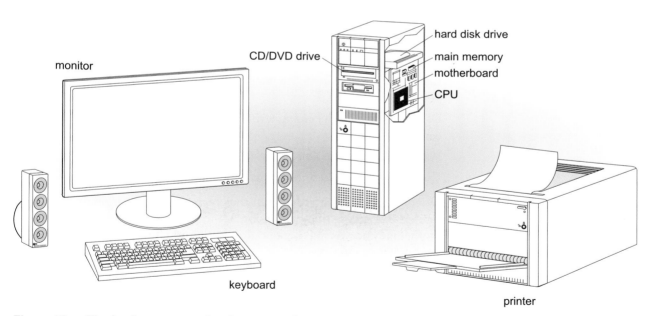

Figure 12   The basic components of a personal computer

Activity 9 (exploratory)

To end this session I would like you to watch a 15-minute video called 'Computers through the generations', which is supplied in the resources page associated with this part on the TU100 website and is also available on DVD. This shows computers from each of the four generations and will hopefully give you a feel for how the physical form of a computer has altered over the years.

Whilst watching the video you should note the purpose and power consumption of the various computers and be able to identify which generation each computer represents. Also, note the physical size of each machine – would it fit in your living room? Is there a relationship between size and power consumption?

2.5 Conclusion

In this session I have outlined some of the major stages and trends in the development of computers up to the 1990s: the technologies that drove the first four generations of computers, the key advantages gained in moving from one technology to the next, and the main kinds of computers in each generation and the tasks to which they were typically put. I hope you can see that the history of computers is also a history of increasing complexity, as more and more manufacturers emerged onto the market.

This session should have helped you with the following learning outcomes.

- List some milestones in the history of computing, including that of the personal computer.
- Describe some of the characteristics of the four generations of computers.
- Perform simple calculations related to energy consumption.
- Take notes as an aid to learning.

In Session 4 I will say a little about the emergence of the modern personal computer. But before that, in Session 3, I'm going to look at the phenomenon known as exponential growth and its relevance to the development of computers.

Smaller, faster, cheaper

3

In this short session I'm going to introduce you to an amazing prediction about the rate of development of computer components, made as early as 1965. This will require you to learn a little about the numerical concept of *exponents*. I will then indicate the wider relevance of exponents to computing by explaining how they are used when representing computer speeds.

Timings
This session should take you around one hour to complete.

3.1 Moore's law

Computers today are smaller, faster and cheaper than they have ever been. As you learned in the last session, I could have made this statement at pretty much any time over the last 30 years and it would have been true; it's doubtful that any other product has maintained such rapid development over such a long period of time. But just how fast has computer development been? In 1965 Gordon Moore, the founder of the giant Intel Corporation, wrote in *Electronics* magazine that he expected the density of electronic components in an integrated circuit to double every year for at least the next ten years.

Density here means the number of components in a given area of a silicon chip.

Activity 10 (self-assessment)

(a) In which generation of computers did Moore make his prediction? —
(b) What technological development led this generation into the next? —

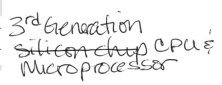
3rd Generation
~~Silicon chip~~ CPU &
Microprocessor

Whether we look at the CPU or at memory, the fundamental component of the computer is the transistor and it has been since the emergence of the second generation. The incorporation of many transistors onto a single silicon chip, in the form of an integrated circuit, started a process of miniaturisation that continues to this day. More and more transistors are placed in a given space; as the distance between the transistors shrinks, so the speed of communication between them increases and the cost per transistor falls.

When he made his prediction, Moore felt that he could see how the technologies needed to achieve it would evolve for the next five to ten years. In fact the prediction was slightly out, as the density of components has doubled every two years rather than the year that was the rate in 1965, and it is this rate of growth that is now associated with Moore.

You will often see Moore's law quoted as doubling every 18 months. In fact the figure does vary a little over time and should only be taken as a rough guide.

Nevertheless, it is quite astonishing that development continues at this rate more than 45 years after the initial prediction. In fact, behind this lies a massive amount of investment to ensure that the trend continues. At some point *Moore's law*, as it is called, moved from being a prediction to being the target for an industry.

The graphs in Figure 13 show two different representations of Moore's law. In both cases the horizontal *axis* shows elapsed time and the vertical axis the number of components (how many transistors will fit on a given area of silicon). However, in graph (b) the vertical axis is calibrated differently; that is, its scale is different.

Activity 11 (exploratory)

Look at the two vertical axes and describe the difference in your own words. Can you say why graph (b) is a more useful representation than graph (a)?

Comment

Here's my attempt. The difference is that on the vertical axis of graph (a) the increments are in a linear sequence (10 000, 20 000, 30 000, etc.), but for graph (b) the increments increase in multiples of ten (10, 100, 1000, etc.).

Graph (a) is useful in that it gives a visual indication of the growth rate, but it's very hard to read off the small values before the year 2000. Graph (b) is easier to read and can be used to predict future values; we call this type of prediction *extrapolation*.

A scale on which the increments increase in multiples of a fixed amount (ten in this case) is referred to as a *logarithmic scale*, and any graph that has such a scale along one of its axes is described as *logarithmic*. Graphs of this type are very widely used to represent data that varies over a large range. When you look at a graph, it's well worth checking whether any of the scales are logarithmic – it is easy to overlook this and so misunderstand the way the data is varying.

The legend of the Ambalapuzha Paal Payasam

To help you appreciate the significance of the doubling in performance every two years suggested by Moore's law, I'd like you to think about the ancient legend of the Ambalapuzha Paal Payasam. In this legend the god Krishna (in disguise of course!) plays chess with a King. The terms of the wager are that the loser should pay in rice, by placing one grain of rice to correspond to the first square of the chessboard, two grains to the second, four to the third and so on – each time doubling the number of grains of rice placed on the previous square. Inevitably, the King agrees to the wager and loses.

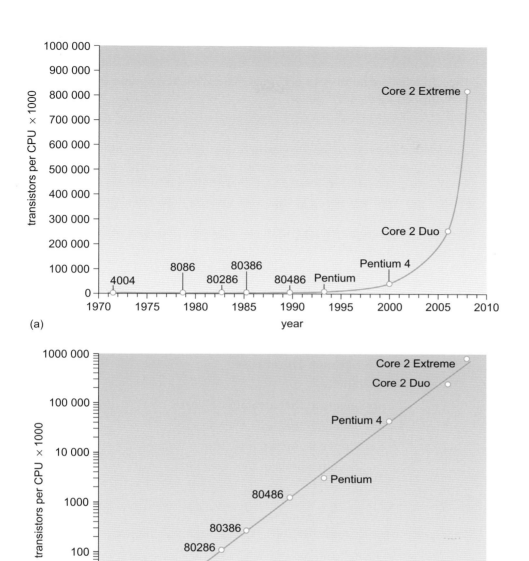

Figure 13   Two different representations of Moore's law

There are 64 squares on a chessboard. By the time the King is placing rice corresponding to the 21st square he requires over a million grains (this is 2 multiplied by itself 20 times). At the 64th square it is almost meaningless to talk in terms of grains of rice, but the total amount required for the board weighs over four hundred billion tonnes.

Activity 12 (self-assessment)

Explain why the number of grains of rice on the 21st square is 2 multiplied by itself 20 times.

This legend goes some way towards showing how remarkable it is that the computer industry doubles the number of components in a given area every two years. And it doesn't stop there. Alongside the development of these components come a host of other developments in communications and magnetic storage media (some of which you will see in a later part) that have at times matched, and even occasionally outstripped, the integrated circuits to which Gordon Moore was referring.

Exponential growth

Moore's law and the legend of the Ambalapuzha Paal Payasam both illustrate *exponential growth*. In both cases, the result at each step is the previous result multiplied by 2. So, for Moore's law we start with the area occupied by one component, then multiply the number of components by 2 for each two-year period. Thus I have:

1 component initially

$1 \times 2 = 2$ components in that area after 2 years

$2 \times 2 = 4$ components in that area after 4 years

$2 \times 2 \times 2 = 8$ components in that area after 6 years

$2 \times 2 \times 2 \times 2 = 16$ components in that area after 8 years

and so on.

A more efficient way of writing the numbers above is as 2^1, 2^2, 2^3, 2^4, etc. That is, we write 2^n to mean '$2 \times 2 \times \ldots \times 2$' with n 2s, where n is any whole number greater than 0. The superscript number beside the 2 is called the *exponent* or *power*; a number that can be written in the form 2^n is called an *exponent of 2* or *power of 2*. So 2, 4, 8, 16, etc. are all powers of 2, since:

2^1 is just 2

2^2 is 2×2, i.e. $2^2 = 4$

2^3 is $2 \times 2 \times 2$, i.e. $2^3 = 8$

2^4 is $2 \times 2 \times 2 \times 2$, i.e. $2^4 = 16$

and so on.

We say that a quantity increases *exponentially* if it can be described using numbers that involve exponents. You've seen that Moore's law is an example of exponential growth – in this case, after n lots of 2 years, the number of components in an area that originally contained just one component is 2^n.

Activity 13 (self-assessment)

Based on the number of components in a given area doubling every 2 years, how many components would there be in an area that originally contained one component after 16 years? You may wish to use a calculator for this activity.

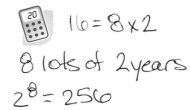

16 = 8 × 2

8 lots of 2 years

$2^8 = 256$

Of course, exponential growth is not limited to powers of 2. In different cases of exponential growth, powers of other numbers can be involved. So, more generally, we write x^n to mean 'x multiplied by itself n times'. For example:

$$3^2 = 3 \times 3 = 9$$

$$4^3 = 4 \times 4 \times 4 = 64$$

$$10^2 = 10 \times 10 = 100$$

Activity 14 (self-assessment)

Find the value of each of the following: 2^6, 2^9, 10^3, 10^4, 8^3. You may wish to use a calculator for this activity.

$2^6 = 64$ $10^4 = 10.000$

$2^9 = 512$ $8^3 = 512$

$10^3 = 1000$

Exponential notation – the use of numbers involving exponents – is very useful, and you will come across it occasionally in TU100. Furthermore, its use extends beyond computing; almost any subject that involves very large numbers, including astronomy, chemistry and finance, uses powers of 10 to express the number of zeros.

Activity 15 (self-assessment)

You've seen that $10^2 = 100$, $10^3 = 1000$ and $10^4 = 10\,000$.

(a) What is 10^5?   *100 000*

(b) Can you explain the pattern?   *count zeros*

(c) Write 1 000 000 as a power of 10.   *— 10^6*

So, for example, rather than writing one hundred thousand billion or 100 000 000 000 000, I could simply write 10^{14}. This notation also reduces the risk of miscounting zeros. You might recall that in order to bail out the banks in the 2008 financial crisis, the UK government made a payment of 400 billion pounds. Since 400 billion is equal to $4 \times 100\,000\,000\,000$, this can be written more simply as 4×10^{11} pounds.

It also makes sense to talk about powers that are negative, zero or fractional (such as 2^{-3}, 10^0 or $5^{1/4}$). For example, any number (except 0) to the power of 0 is 1. You will learn more about negative powers of 10 and how they can be used to express very small numbers in a later part.

Eventually, exponential growth always has to stop because it encounters some physical limit, be it the availability of grains of rice or of atoms in a silicon chip. The fact that this has not yet happened in the computing industry is remarkable, but how long can it be before we reach a point where it is impossible to make things any smaller? We might encounter such a limit because it is not possible to manufacture components smaller than a certain size – less than an atom wide, say – or because the components wouldn't function reliably below a certain size. On the other hand, people have been saying this for many years but still Moore's law continues to apply.

3.2   How fast?

The speed of modern computers is difficult to quantify, because the speed of a computer depends on the nature of the task it is performing and because different machines are optimised for different tasks. However, a common approach is to identify the number of instructions that the CPU can carry out in a given interval of time, often one second. Very large numbers are involved, usually expressed as powers of 10. For example, you will hear the terms *gigaflops* (which shortens to *Gflops*) and *teraflops* (*Tflops*) used in this context. The 'flops' part stands for 'floating-point operations per second', while the prefixes 'giga' and 'tera' indicate the power of 10 involved: giga indicates 10^9 (or a billion) and tera indicates 10^{12}.

You can, very roughly, think of floating-point operations as operations that use numbers.

Activity 16 (self-assessment)

Earlier in this part, when you looked at power consumption, you came across the idea that a kilowatt is equal to a thousand watts. The prefix 'kilo' is a common one – what power of 10 do you think it indicates?

10^3

Inevitably, given Moore's law, when talking about computers we need larger numbers than we encounter in the everyday world. Table 2 shows a list of commonly used prefixes and their abbreviations.

Table 2 Prefixes and their abbreviations

Prefix	Abbreviation	Multiply by …	Power of 10
kilo	k	1000	10^3
mega	M	1000 000	10^6
giga	G	1000 000 000	10^9
tera	T	1000 000 000 000	10^{12}
peta	P	1000 000 000 000 000	10^{15}
exa	E	1000 000 000 000 000 000	10^{18}
zetta	Z	1000 000 000 000 000 000 000	10^{21}
yotta	Y	1000 000 000 000 000 000 000 000	10^{24}

Note that for each prefix except for 'kilo', the abbreviation is a capital letter.

At the time of writing (2010), the main prefixes in everyday use are the first four: kilo, mega, giga and tera. The speed of a typical personal computer might be tens of gigaflops. Supercomputers are capable of reaching speeds of just over one petaflop.

The prefixes shown in Table 2 can be used not just for computer speed but in any other situation involving large numbers – for example, when measuring power (kilowatts, megawatts, etc.). However, in Session 6 you will learn that when applied to computer memory, these prefixes don't have exactly the same meanings as those given in Table 2.

In addition to prefixes to cover large scales there are also prefixes to cover very small scales, which you may already have seen in use. For example, 'milli' (abbreviation m) means 'divide by 1000' and 'micro' (abbreviation μ) means 'divide by 1000 000'. You will learn more about these prefixes in a later part.

3.3 Conclusion

In this session I introduced you to Moore's law, which is an example of exponential growth. I then looked at exponential notation more generally, before considering the prefixes that are commonly used to describe large powers of 10.

This session should have helped you with the following learning outcomes.

- Explain the concept of exponential growth.
- Work with exponential notation in simple contexts, and with prefixes for large numbers such as kilo, mega and giga.

The next session returns to the history of computer development to look at the emergence of the modern personal computer.

4 Computers as we know them

Timings
This session should take you around two hours to complete.

I'm going to start this session by considering some of the more recent history of today's personal computers, leading on from the discussion in Session 2. I'll then explain how today's use of computers goes far beyond this vision of one person and their machine, to a world of *ubiquitous computing* in which computers are all around us. I'll finish by introducing you to the emerging concept of *cloud computing*.

This session should provide you with a good foundation for later parts of TU100, when you will look at both ubiquitous computing and cloud computing in more depth.

4.1 Personal computers

You saw in Part 1 that personal computers have come to play a hugely important role in society. In Session 2 I presented a brief history of personal computers, from their emergence in the 1970s to the more modern machines of the 1990s. These early personal computers were the ancestors of those we are familiar with today; developments in technology led to reductions in their cost and size, putting them within the reach of more and more people. But why did more and more people actually want to use computers? Aside from technology, just what propelled the development of the personal computers that many of us use every day? I will discuss three key factors: killer apps, increasing usability, and the rise of the internet.

Killer apps

VisiCalc was a forerunner of Excel. It was produced by Software Arts.

A *killer app* is any application considered so desirable that people would purchase a computer purely to use it. One of the first killer apps was the spreadsheet application VisiCalc, which was released in 1979 for the Apple II computer. VisiCalc had a massive impact on sales of the Apple II – not surprisingly, sales to the financial sector were colossal. A similar thing happened with the launch of Lotus 1-2-3 (another spreadsheet application) for the IBM PC. Software became the key to marketing personal computers.

Interestingly, though, exactly how software would come to dominate and steer the market was not widely understood in the 1980s. When IBM launched the 5150 personal computer in 1981, they gave it what was described as *open architecture*; this meant that IBM made public various elements of the computer's design. The aim was to enable other companies to produce software and peripheral devices, and thus to ensure that there were plenty of useful things the machine could do. Yet this open architecture approach eventually led to two things that IBM didn't foresee:

You will learn more about open architecture and IBM in a later part.

1   It enabled other companies to produce clone machines at a fraction of the price that were able to run the same software as their IBM counterparts.

2   It enabled Microsoft, who produced the operating system for the IBM machine, to dominate the software market, because this operating system was used on all the clone machines as well.

With so many manufacturers all producing compatible machines, the software market for games and office applications boomed. To this day there remain two dominant types of personal computer: Microsoft Windows-based machines, which are derivatives of the IBM clones, and Apple machines, which retain a smaller share of the market.

Increasing usability

All computers have an operating system, which can be thought of as mediating between the user and the electronics of the machine. The operating system manages the computer's different hardware components and peripheral devices, provides a means for the user to interact with the computer, and organises the running of application software (see Figure 14). You will probably be familiar with your computer's operating system – perhaps Microsoft's Windows or Apple's Mac OS X. Because it facilitates your interaction with your computer, the operating system makes a crucial contribution to your computer's *usability* – put simply, how easy it is to use.

Activity 17 (exploratory)

Identify your computer's operating system (and version number if it has one). If you are not sure, watch your screen next time you start up your computer; the operating system information is usually one of the first things to appear.

Comment
While writing this I'm using a Linux operating system called Ubuntu version 8.04.

Over the years, operating systems have grown increasingly sophisticated. Their key development in terms of usability was probably the *graphical user interface (GUI)*, which was first seen on the Apple Lisa machine of the early 1980s. This enabled users to interact with graphics on the

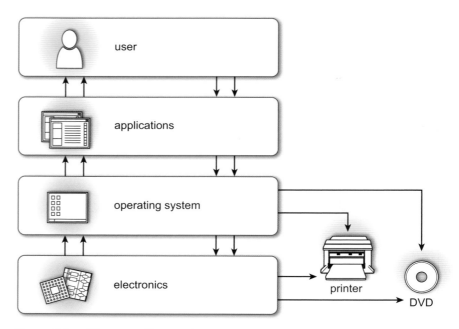

Figure 14   The operating system

GUI is pronounced goo-ee. The first GUI was developed by Alan Kay and Douglas Engelbart. You will learn more about GUIs and their development in a later part.

computer screen by pointing and clicking using a mouse. Before that it had been necessary to remember a series of command codes, which had to be typed into a text-based *command-line interface*, in order to do anything. Thus the GUI represented a huge step forward in usability. Figure 15 shows the difference in appearance between a command-line interface and a GUI.

Activity 18 (exploratory)

So what was the world of computing like before the emergence of GUIs? If your computer is running Windows then you can still use the old command-line environment, which requires you to enter command codes to communicate with the computer, by opening a Command Prompt window.

(a) Open a command-line environment on your computer as follows:

For Windows Vista click on Start, then Programs, then Command Prompt.

For Windows 7 and XP click on Start, then All Programs, then Accessories, then Command Prompt.

When the Command Prompt window opens you will see a line that starts something like:

C:\Users\... or C:\Documents and Settings\...

(b) Type help and press the Return key. This will list the commands and what they do.

(a)

(b)

Figure 15   (a) A command-line interface; (b) a GUI

(c) Type color help (note the US spelling) and press the Return key. See
if you can work out how to turn the text in the Command Prompt
window light yellow and the background purple.

(d) Close the Command Prompt window by typing exit and pressing the
Return key.

Comment

To turn the text light yellow and the background purple, type color 5E.
(To set it back to the default, just type color; alternatively, it will
automatically reset itself when you close the Command Prompt window.)

If you're not running a machine that is able to do this activity, Figure 16
provides a pair of screenshots to show what you would have seen.

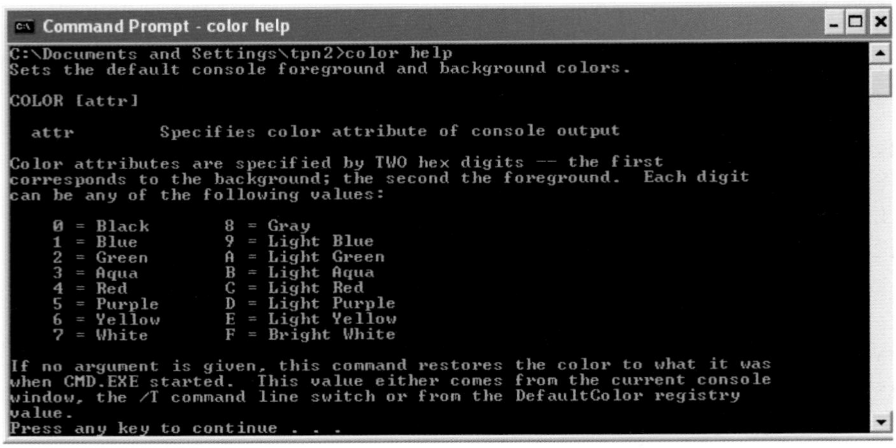

(a)

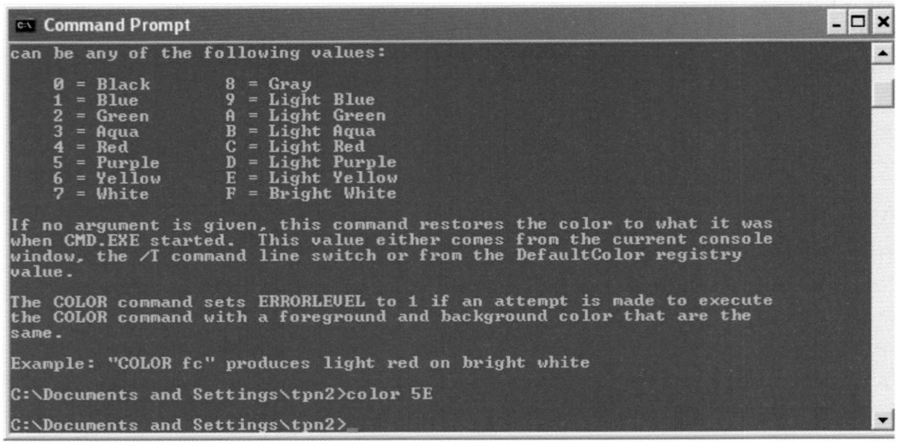

(b)

Figure 16   The Command Prompt window: (a) with default colour settings; (b) with altered colour settings

The rise of the internet

The internet has its origins in a 1969 research project known as the Advanced Research Project Agency network or ARPANET, which you will learn more about in a later part. However, the internet as we know it emerged in the 1980s and grew in public popularity with the birth of the Web in 1992. The personal computer industry was driven in a new direction, as connectedness gradually became essential. Today most personal computers rely on being connected to the internet to maintain their integrity, using it to update virus scanners or the operating system. This assumption of connectedness, as you will see later when I discuss cloud computing, is leading to a very different future for the personal computer.

4.2 The rest of the iceberg

Activity 19 (exploratory)

Before you start to read this section, think back to yesterday. Spend a few minutes making a brief list of any computers you interacted with over the course of the day, and estimate roughly how many of them there were. I'll return to this shortly.

When asked what a computer looks like, most people today think of a personal computer (Figure 17). The image they have is probably of a machine equipped with a keyboard and a monitor; it may or may not be a portable machine such as a laptop computer. A smaller number of people might first think of a dedicated games console. Again, these are fairly recognisable as computers – at least they still have a monitor! Yet although games consoles and personal computers are the most visible and versatile (and most lucrative) kinds of computers, they're not the most common. In fact, you may be surprised to learn that they probably represent less than 2% of the computers in the world!

Examples of games consoles are Sony's PSP, Nintendo's Wii and Microsoft's Xbox.

After personal computers and games consoles, you might nominate the apparently omnipresent mobile phone as the next candidate in the computer popularity contest. Your mobile phone may well include the facility to browse the Web and run games programs, in which case it is certainly a computer – and it has a monitor and a kind of keyboard, too. But even mobile phones are not the most common kind of computer. By far the most common computers are those referred to as *embedded*.

An *embedded computer* is one that controls a specific device and that has usually been designed to carry out a highly specialised function. A vast range of devices contain embedded computers, so the chances are that you have interacted with a large number of them today. For example, you may have used a bank card in a chip and pin system at the shops, or switched

Figure 17   What most people think of as a computer

Any car built in the last ten years or so will contain several embedded computers.

on your microwave oven, or driven your car, or used a swipe card to access a building or service. Did you buy a cup of coffee from an automatic vending machine? All of these examples involve highly dedicated computers – embedded computers that may have neither keyboards nor monitors.

Each embedded computer is programmed to carry out a specific task or range of tasks. For example, your chip and pin card holds information about your bank account. When you insert it into an ATM (cashpoint) it enables you to communicate with your bank. Both the card and the ATM contain computers. However, note that the embedded computers I have described in these examples might not fit everyone's definition of a computer, since user interaction with them is tightly constrained. For this reason some people prefer to refer to them as *microcontrollers* or *microprocessors* rather than computers.

As well as the large number of embedded computers that can be found all around you, if you went online to use the Web today then you probably interacted with many more computers that you were quite unaware of: computers such as *web servers*, which respond to requests for web pages.

Activity 20 (self-assessment)

In the light of what you have read since Activity 19, return to the list of computers that you interacted with yesterday and update it. Remember that you're only asked for a rough estimate of the number of such computers.

Activity 21 (self-assessment)

Figure 18 shows a timeline on which I have identified a few of the more significant developments in computing and related technologies over the last 60 years. Take a little time to add in some of your own, based on your study of Session 2 and Session 4.

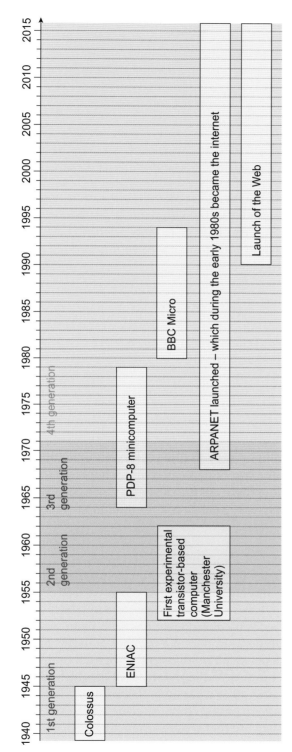

Figure 18   **Timeline showing some significant developments in computing**

4.3   Into the future …

The examples I've just been considering all add up to one fact: computers are everywhere around us, increasingly influencing all sorts of aspects of our lives. They are also increasingly 'invisible', in that we are often unaware of their presence and indeed of their interactions with each other.

Ubiquitous computing

The term *ubiquitous computing* describes the idea that computers are becoming *pervasive* – that is, they are integrated into the world around us. The term was coined by Mark Weiser at the Xerox Palo Alto Research Center (better known as Xerox PARC). It was at Xerox PARC that many of the most significant developments in the field of computing took place, including the mouse and the GUI, laser printing and SmallTalk, the software language behind Sense (the programming environment you will use as part of TU100). The following quotations explain what Weiser meant by ubiquitous computing.

> Ubiquitous computing names the third wave in computing, just now beginning. First were mainframes, each shared by lots of people. Now we are in the personal computing era, person and machine staring uneasily at each other across the desktop. Next comes ubiquitous computing, or the age of *calm technology*, when technology recedes into the background of our lives.

> Weiser, 1996

> [Ubiquitous computing] will bring information technology beyond the big problems like corporate finance and school homework, to the little annoyances like Where are the car-keys, Can I get a parking place, and Is that shirt I saw last week at Macy's still on the rack?

> Weiser and Brown, 1996

The four generations of computer described in Session 2 were identified using the technologies they were based on, i.e. valves, transistors, integrated circuits and microprocessors. When we talk of ubiquitous computing, we move to a different perspective in which we begin to categorise technologies by our interactions with them. As you have seen already, early computers supported a number of users; subsequently computers became personal; more recently, we each find ourselves interacting with a number of computers, each of which may itself interact with other people and other computers (Figure 19). Often we are not even aware of where data is coming from or where it is stored – and more than this, we're often unaware that we are interacting with computers at all. Ubiquitous computing is clearly already with us.

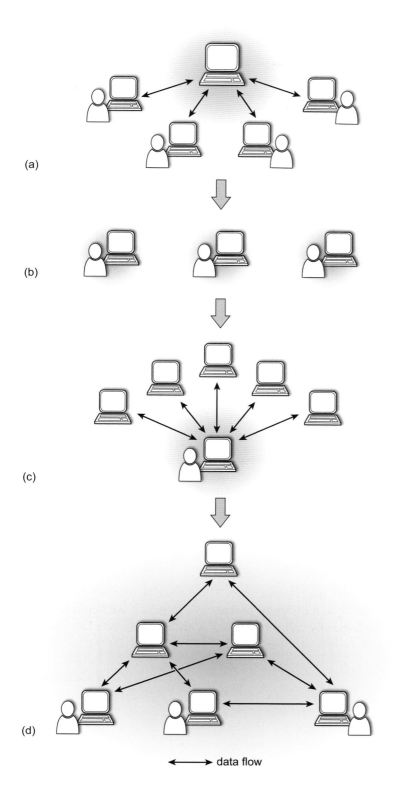

(a)

(b)

(c)

(d)

◀——▶ data flow

Figure 19   The different interactions between people and computers: (a) many people interacting with a single computer; (b) people each interacting with their own computer; (c) individual interacting with many computers; (d) many individuals and many computers all interacting

Calm technology

Calm technology takes ubiquitous computing to a new level. The term describes a form of ubiquitous computing in which technology supports our daily activities but is more or less imperceptible. This indicates a direction of development for ubiquitous computing that is not yet fully achieved, but that is seen by many people as a desirable outcome.

> The most potentially interesting, challenging, and profound change implied by the ubiquitous computing era is a focus on *calm*. If computers are everywhere they better stay out of the way, and that means designing them so that the people being shared by the computers remain serene and in control.
>
> Weiser and Brown, 1996

As an example of calm technology, consider a microwave oven. You can set all sorts of parameters – clock time, cooking time, defrost time, intensity – and indeed you have to set at least some of these each time you want to cook your food. But suppose the oven were capable of determining all these parameters for itself, without your input: it might receive a radio signal with the time of day, perhaps read packaging on the food to identify cooking time and intensity, and even measure the food's temperature to gauge whether defrosting was required. You would simply have to insert the food, then walk away and await a call on your mobile phone telling you that your meal was ready. Most of the technology behind what was happening would be totally invisible to you; all you would need to do is select the food and place it in the microwave.

You can see from the Weiser and Brown quotation above that the notion of calm technology has been around for quite a while. You can also see from the microwave example, which might seem in the realm of fantasy, that we still have a long way to go!

In fact, there are many examples of calm technology already in existence, but because they're 'calm' we have to stop and look for them. At Xerox PARC, one of the first examples of calm technology to be developed was a device to measure how busy the computer network was. It consisted of a small electric motor connected to a piece of string, which dangled freely in the room. The motor was set up to rotate at varying speeds depending on how much traffic was on the network, which in turn made the string jiggle about. This enabled people to see how busy the network was at a glance, without having to interpret a readout. It's this notion of the information being there but not intruding that is key to the idea of calm technology.

Activity 22 (exploratory)

Describe an instance of calm technology that you have observed or used. If you are not aware of any then can you identify an area of your life, along the lines of the microwave example above, where there is potential for calm technology?

Comment

My car, like many these days, has traction control. If the wheels lose their grip because the road surface is too slippery, an electronic system interferes to apply the brakes and/or reduce the power to the driving wheels. Aside from a flickering light on the dashboard, I am unaware that a computer is mediating my driving. This enables me to get on with driving the car without having to exert unnecessary effort to control it or even noticing that it is being controlled.

Calm technology is really about technology not being intrusive, thus allowing us to relax (feel calm) in its presence. This doesn't mean the technology has to be invisible, but it shouldn't give (or ask for) more information than is necessary. However, if we want to stay out of the loop then we have to be prepared to allow data exchange to take place – and this may have consequences, not least for data security.

Some people would be very happy for technology to be almost invisible, but this does imply a certain loss of control; the technology has to make decisions that would otherwise have been yours. In the microwave cooking example, there seem few disadvantages in letting the machine take control – although if you prefer your soup lukewarm rather than hot, you might want to vary the cooking time occasionally – but it isn't hard to imagine other situations in which the disadvantages could be more severe.

Cloud computing

For many businesses and individuals, the financial overheads of computing can be very high; they may need to invest in and upgrade hardware and software that they don't use regularly. However, the interconnectedness of modern computers offers an alternative approach, one that involves the sharing of software and hardware over the internet. This is known as *cloud computing*. All the storage capacity and processing power is provided remotely, from the 'cloud' – the internet. Under such a model you might pay for computing facilities in much the same way that you pay for utilities such as gas or electricity (Figure 20), enabling you to pay only for what you use. From this concept comes the term *utility computing*, which is often used interchangeably with cloud computing (though in fact the two terms have slightly different meanings, as you will see in a later part).

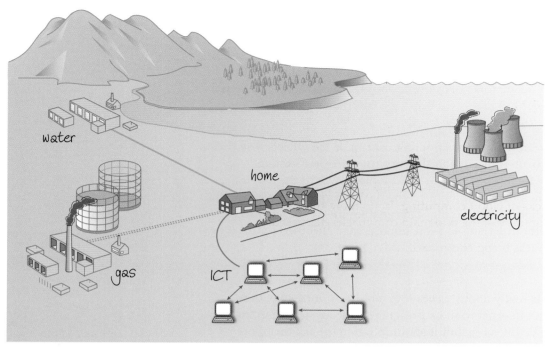

Figure 20   **Computing as a utility**

For example, take a small publishing company consisting of ten staff, perhaps producing a magazine. The staff could be working on a large number of articles in a variety of ways, so the applications they would need to use might include:

- word processors to write articles
- a database to store and retrieve articles
- spreadsheets for accounting.

They would also want to be able to share articles – authors might want to collaborate with each other, or share a document with an editor, so this facility could be vital. In addition, the company would need to be sure that its data – articles, financial information, etc. – was safe. This means having a place to store the data. Since the office could potentially be lost if there were a fire, it would be best to have a remote site as a store for vital information. At certain times the company might need to store large amounts of data, while at others it might have much smaller data storage requirements. Finally, some of the software it requires might be used only rarely – spreadsheet applications for a yearly audit, for example.

Given all these requirements, if the company were to follow the traditional model then there's a good chance it would have to employ a full-time person to look after its IT – and for a company of ten people, this is quite an overhead! Then, in addition, there is the cost of equipment replacement and software. For these reasons, the cloud seems an excellent option for this company. Employees could connect using their personal computers from anywhere in the world and have access to the latest applications as well as share articles. The company would not have to purchase and maintain a network, and would not need to employ a specialist to look after its IT systems.

Certainly the cloud model offers greater freedom to expand whilst apparently reducing hardware, software and energy costs and increasing reliability. But are there other, hidden issues?

Activity 23 (self-assessment)

Read the article in Box 3, in which the author reveals what he sees as the potential drawbacks of cloud computing. In no more than a couple of sentences each, summarise the two main drawbacks discussed.

Note that when you read or view materials, it is vital that you pay attention to the perspectives of the author(s). It's fairly obvious in the case of a commercial company that the materials may have a bias – after all, they're probably trying to sell you something – but that's not the only motive that might influence the objectivity of an article. If it's a press article, for example, it could be trying to sensationalise the facts in order to sell more papers.

In places in the following article, the author uses quite emotive language: language that draws you into feeling something about what you are reading. This is not a flaw in the article; it would be very dull if articles were written in such a way that the reader was unable to have some emotional response. But as a student, you need to maintain an awareness of the author's perspective and of how you are being drawn in. This is a subject that you will return to in a later part. When you read this article, watch how the author colours your thinking with references to 'the Hound of the Baskervilles'.

Ethics

I hope you can see from Activity 23 that there are some interesting debates emerging about the rights and wrongs of how we use ICT and computers. Do you take the view that the state should have the right to look at your information? If so, what about the security forces from another country?

You will return to the subject of ethics in a later part.

There is an ethical dimension to nearly every technology, whether it is stem-cell research, weapons development or satellite TV. The decisions we make about the application of these technologies depend not only on technical feasibility but also on our values and beliefs. You can probably see already that ethics is a pervasive subject and something that, as a student in this field, you can't ignore.

Box 3 Storm warning for cloud computing

My friend Simon is one of those net entrepreneurs with the attention to detail it takes to have an idea and turn it into an effective company. He's currently on his second job search service, and it seems to be going very well.

One reason for the success may be that Simon has embraced the network age with a dedication that most of us can only wonder at. He uses a range of productivity tools, scheduling services and collaborative systems to manage both his personal and professional life, and once confessed to me that he had "outsourced his memory" to Microsoft Outlook and its calendar service.

Recently I've noticed that Simon's head is in the cloud. Or rather, his business is, as he and his team have moved most of their systems online, taking advantage of the move from local storage and processing to cloud computing, where data and services are provided online and accessed from a PC or any other device.

For a small but growing business it means that new storage and processing capacity can be added incrementally instead of having to buy a whole new server at a time.

And for a distributed company like WorkCircle, where the team all work from their own homes or offices, it makes coordination, document sharing and collaboration a lot easier.

The approach is growing in popularity, and Google, Microsoft and Amazon are among the many large companies working on ways to attract users to their offerings, with Google Apps, Microsoft's Live Mesh and Amazon S3 all signing up customers as they try to figure out what works and what can turn a profit.

The technical obstacles to making distributed systems work are formidable, and while books like Nick Carr's The Big Switch talk optimistically about the potential for utility computing to be offered to homes and businesses just like electric power, building robust, reliable and scalable systems around these new models will tax our ingenuity.

Constant outages

As we become more reliant on the cloud any problems will become more severe, as we can see in the irritation that many users feel with Twitter at the moment because of constant outages, dropped messages and general flakiness as the company tries to cope with what was clearly an unanticipated growth in usage.

It would be a lot worse if your spreadsheets or presentations were inaccessible because of problems in the cloud, or rather because of problems with the physical computers or network connections that make cloud computing possible.

Because behind all the rhetoric and promotional guff the 'cloud' is no such thing: every piece of data is stored on a physical hard drive or in solid state memory, every instruction is processed by a physical computer and every network interaction connects two locations in the real world.

It is often useful to conceptualise online activities as cyberspace, the place behind the screen, but the internet is firmly of the real world, and that is one of the greatest problems facing cloud computing today.

In the real world national borders, commercial rivalries and political imperatives all come into play, turning the cloud into a miasma as heavy with menace as the fog over the Grimpen Mire that concealed the Hound of the Baskervilles in Arthur Conan Doyle's story.

The issue was recently highlighted by reports that the Canadian government has a policy of not allowing public sector IT projects to use US-based hosting services because of concerns over data protection.

Under the US Patriot Act the FBI and other agencies can demand to see content stored on any computer, even if it [is] being hosted on behalf of another sovereign state.

If your data hosting company gets a National Security Letter then not only do they have to hand over the information, they are forbidden from telling you or anyone else – apart from their lawyer – about it.

The Canadians are rather concerned about this, and rightly so. According to the US-based Electronic Frontier Foundation, a civil liberties group that helped the Internet Archive successfully challenge an NSL, more than 200,000 were issued between 2003 and 2006, and the chances are that Google, Microsoft and Amazon were on the recipient list.

Encrypting data

Even encrypting the data stored in data centres won't always work, as one of the benefits of Amazon's S3 and other services is that they do remote processing too, and the data needs to be decrypted before that can happen.

This is not just a US issue, of course, although attention has focused on the US because that is where most of the cloud data centres can be found. It applies just as much to the UK, where the Regulation of Investigatory Powers Act will allow the police or

Encrypting data involves using secret codes to transform it, aiming to protect it from prying eyes. You will learn more about encryption in a later part.

secret services to demand access to databases and servers. And other countries may lack even the thin veneer of democratic oversight that the USA and UK offer to the surveillance activities of their intelligence agencies.

Companies have no real choice but to comply with the law in countries where they operate, and I don't expect a campaign of civil disobedience from the big hosting providers. Those of us who use the cloud just need to be clear about the realities of the situation – and not send or store anything on GoogleMail or HotMail that the US government might want to use against us.

Part of the attraction of the internet was always that it transcended geographic boundaries of all forms, whether political or physical. Communities grew because people shared interests or values, not because they lived in the same place or were under the same government. It was far from perfect, but it gave us a glimpse of a better world.

The push towards cloud computing may force us to be more realistic about the boundaries that have always existed. Perhaps it is time for the UN to consider a cyberspace rights treaty that will outline what it's acceptable to do when other people's data comes into your jurisdiction.

Source: Thompson, 2008

4.4   Conclusion

From the early days of code-cracking at Bletchley Park that you learned about in Session 2 to issues of state control and security on the internet, computing and ICTs have had and are continuing to have a massive influence on society. So how do they actually work? This is what you'll begin to learn about in the next session.

This session should have helped you with the following learning outcomes.

- List some milestones in the history of computing, including that of the personal computer.
- Identify potential devices in which computers might be embedded.
- Explain the concepts of ubiquitous computing and cloud computing, and identify their ethical dimensions.

The language of computers

5

Having looked at some history, it's now time to lift the lid and see what actually goes on inside a computer. In this session I will introduce you to binary logic, which has become key to the functioning of computers. I'll then explain what binary numbers are and begin to describe their role in representing information inside computers.

Timings
This session should take you around two hours to complete.

5.1 Binary logic

Binary logic underpins most forms of digital technology. It was developed in the mid-nineteenth century by George Boole (Figure 21), an Irish mathematician and philosopher, long before anyone considered making a computer using electronic components. At the time Boole was interested in exploring the fundamental nature of truth, so he developed a system involving symbols – a *symbolic logic* – to help him reason about truth and falsity. This system is often referred to as *Boolean logic* or *binary logic*, and it focuses on the manipulation of 1s and 0s (1 to represent TRUE and 0 to represent FALSE).

When trying to understand the nature of the digital world, it is useful to know something about the binary numbers that Boole based his algebra upon, because binary numbers are the form in which information is held in a computer. As you saw in Session 2, a *binary number* is a sequence of digits, each of which is either 1 or 0. For example, 100011 can be considered as a binary number. When stored in a computer each digit of a binary number is referred to as a *bit*, which is a contraction of the words *binary digit*.

Figure 21   George Boole

There are a number of different ways in which it is possible to represent 1s and 0s in the physical world, the most obvious representation being a switch. In one position (or state) a switch is said to be 'off' (0) and in another 'on' (1) (Figure 22). The valves and transistors that I described earlier are ideal for this role, but there are other options, as Box 4 explains.

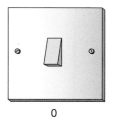
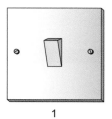

0   1

Figure 22   Using switches to represent 0s and 1s

Box 4 Does it have to be electrical?

Electronics allows us to manufacture large numbers of switches cheaply and to drive them using very little energy, but electronics wasn't always the obvious first choice for computing. For example, in the 1960s it was thought that hydraulic systems might make effective computers, and much time was spent studying the switching of fluids at high speeds. In fact, the performance of these hydraulic switches was comparable to that of the electronic components of the time!

Although this may seem very strange from today's perspective, it does serve to demonstrate that the physical *form* that switches take, be it mechanical, electrical or even hydraulic, can be treated as a separate issue from that of their *function* – that is, the manipulation and storage of bits that can be described using binary logic. For this reason, it was possible for Boole to contribute to the world of computing long before the existence of the first electronic computers.

Even after electronic computers were developed, information was often stored using mechanisms that by today's standards would be considered quite crude. For example, as you learned in Session 2, some early computers used punch cards or paper tape to store data: these were literally cards or paper tape with holes punched in them, with a hole representing 1 and its absence 0 (Figure 23). These could easily be converted to switch states.

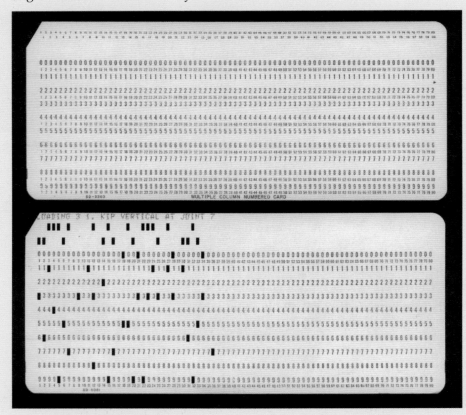

Figure 23   **A punch card**

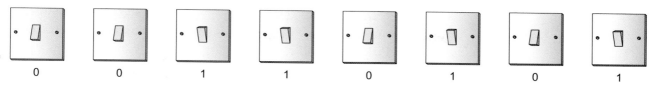

| 0 | 0 | 1 | 1 | 0 | 1 | 0 | 1 |

Figure 24   A row of switches representing an eight-digit binary number

Clearly a single switch isn't going to make the world's most sophisticated logic machine, but what happens if I have more switches? This would allow me to represent several 1s and 0s at the same time – in fact, I can represent any binary number as long as I have enough switches (Figure 24). This is the form in which data is stored, manipulated and transferred in computers.

How many?

You can see from the preceding discussion that the more switches (or bits) I have, the more different binary numbers I can represent. If I use a single bit then I can represent only two different numbers, a 1 or a 0. If I use two bits then I can make four different binary numbers:

00

01

10

11.

Activity 24 (self-assessment)

How many different binary numbers can be made with three bits? To start you off, 000, 001 and 010 are all possibilities.

There's a pattern here that is very like the pattern you met earlier when I discussed Moore's law. Every time I increase the number of bits by one, the number of possible binary numbers doubles. So:

with 1 bit I can form 2 binary numbers

with 2 bits I can form 4 binary numbers, that's 2×2 binary numbers

with 3 bits I can form 8 binary numbers, that's $2 \times 2 \times 2$ binary numbers

with 4 bits I can form 16 binary numbers, that's $2 \times 2 \times 2 \times 2$ binary numbers

and so on. Just as with Moore's law, this pattern can be represented using powers of 2:

$2^1 = 2$

$2^2 = 4$

$2^3 = 8$

$2^4 = 16$

and so on. Here you can see that the number of possible binary numbers that can be made from n bits, where n is any whole number bigger than 0, is 2^n.

Activity 25 (self-assessment)

In computing, a set of eight bits is referred to as a *byte*. How many different binary numbers would I be able to form using a byte?

I now want to take a look at how we might choose to represent the physical world using binary numbers.

5.2 Representation

ICT and computing often rely on representing some aspect of the real world in a form that can be stored, transmitted or manipulated.

Activity 26 (exploratory)

Can you think of an aspect of the real world that might be represented on a computer?

Comment
Sounds – music, for example – can be captured by recording equipment and the recording put on to a computer. That recording represents the real-world sound. Similarly, images from the real world can be captured on camera and put on to a computer.

Analogue and discrete quantities

In general, there are two main ways in which we can represent aspects of the world around us. To understand these, you first need to know about the concept of analogue and discrete quantities.

An *analogue* quantity is one that can take any value in a continuous range of values. For instance, consider temperature: this is a quantity that changes *continuously*. If you heat up a pan of water, the water temperature does not jump instantaneously from one point to another – it does not leap straight from 99 degrees Celsius (°C) to 100 °C, or even from 99.9 °C to 100 °C. Instead, the temperature rises continuously, taking all values up to 100 °C with no gaps or jumps. No matter how small the gap between two temperatures, it is always possible to find another temperature value between them. For this reason, temperature is an analogue quantity.

Conversely, a *discrete* quantity is one that varies in a series of clear steps or that can only have one of a finite set of values. One such discrete quantity is the price of petrol per litre in the UK. This can only take a finite number of values in any given range – for example, between £1.00 and £1.20 the price has to be one of the set of values £1.00, £1.01, £1.02, …, £1.20. In fact, anything that we can count is likely to be a discrete quantity. So the weight of a pile of sand is an analogue quantity, but the number of grains of sand in the pile is discrete.

Activity 27 (self-assessment)

Which quantities in the following list are analogue and which discrete?

1   The population of the UK
2   The amount of heat from a fire
3   The speed of a car
4   The energy of a star
5   The size of the audience at a play
6   The pressure of the atmosphere

Analogue and digital representation

You have learned that temperature is fundamentally an analogue quantity. This can be seen when measuring it using a traditional mercury- or alcohol-in-glass thermometer, as illustrated in Figure 25.

In such a thermometer, the level of the liquid column in the glass tube varies continuously according to the continuous variation in the temperature. Just as the temperature itself can take on any value in a given range, so can the level of the liquid in the thermometer. So in this case the liquid column is an *analogue representation*: the level of the liquid is *analogous* to the temperature. In general, an analogue representation is a representation of an analogue quantity in which the representation varies continuously with the quantity.

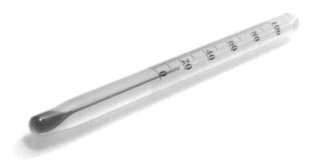

Figure 25   A traditional thermometer

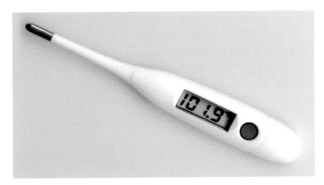

Figure 26   A digital thermometer

There is, however, another way of measuring temperature. We don't have to use liquid in a thermometer; a common alternative method is to use a digital thermometer, as illustrated in Figure 26.

The digital thermometer has a sensor that represents the temperature as an electrical voltage. At this stage, the representation is still analogue and so can take any value of voltage. Yet the digital thermometer must display the temperature as a numerical value in degrees Celsius or Fahrenheit, and to do this it 'converts' the voltage to a discrete quantity using a device called an *analogue to digital converter*. This device takes the continuously varying voltage as an input and outputs a pattern of bits, which are then ascribed numbers and displayed by the thermometer: in essence, it converts from a continuous range of values to a range that varies in discrete steps.

So this kind of thermometer represents temperature as if it were a discrete quantity; in other words, it gives a *digital representation* of temperature. In a digital representation of an analogue quantity, the quantity is approximated with a sequence of discrete values. A digital thermometer would probably display temperatures to the nearest degree – so a temperature of, say, 25.8 °C would appear as 26 °C. Even a more accurate digital thermometer designed for scientific or medical purposes can use only a finite number of digits in its display (for instance, the one shown in Figure 26 is displaying the temperature to the nearest tenth of a degree). Taking a digital representation of an analogue quantity usually involves some loss of accuracy.

Figure 27 shows two temperature plots on the same axes: one a plot of a continuously varying temperature, and the other the corresponding series of discrete values that might come from a digital thermometer. You can see from this figure that the two plots are quite different.

Of course, discrete quantities by their nature normally demand digital representations. For instance, Morse code is a digital representation of the characters of the English language in which three values (the symbols dot, dash and space) can be used to code any message (Figure 28).

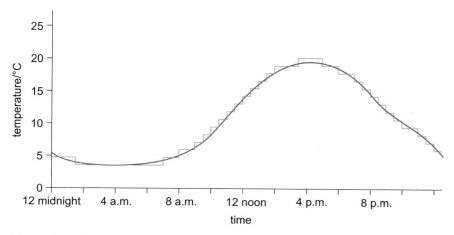

Figure 27   Analogue and digital temperature plots on the same axes

A · —   1 · — — — —

B — · · ·   2 · · — — —

C — · — ·   3 · · · — —

D — · ·   4 · · · · —

E ·   5 · · · · ·

Figure 28   Part of the Morse code

Activity 28 (self-assessment)

What are the essential differences between analogue and digital representations?

Activity 29 (self-assessment)

I've shown you how temperature, an analogue quantity, can be given a digital representation. Can you think of another example of a digital representation of an analogue quantity?

One key factor in the rise of digital communication and data storage is that almost any analogue quantity (from a voltage or a current to a sound pressure wave or the colour of a light) can, in principle, be represented digitally. This in turn means that the representation can be stored and manipulated by a computer, with the values of the digital representation being 'coded' by binary numbers stored in the computer. You will learn more about what this coding involves in the next session.

(a) If I use one byte, how many different discrete values can I represent? (Recall your answer to Activity 25.)

(b) I want to measure temperatures from 1 °C up to 100 °C within half a degree accuracy. Can I do this with one byte?

5.3 Conclusion

In this session I've introduced an important example of how information about the real world can be represented in terms of binary numbers – namely, how real-world temperatures can be represented discretely and, ultimately, in binary form. In the next session I will explain how any number in the real world can be represented in binary form.

This session should have helped you with the following learning outcomes.

• Describe how binary numbers are stored in a computer.

• Contrast analogue and digital quantities and representations.

• Describe how the physical world can be represented in digital form.

Counting in binary

6

The first computers were designed as calculating machines, and performing calculations – often involving very large numbers – is still a vital computing task. But how does your computer begin to work out even a simple numerical calculation? In this session I will explain how computers store numbers by representing them in binary form.

Timings
This session should take you around two hours to complete.

> If it has been a while since you did any numerical calculations then you may want to take this session slowly, perhaps going over it more than once. Do take time to try the activities for yourself.

6.1 Decimal numbers

In the everyday world we use a system of counting and arithmetic that relies on having ten different symbols for digits, i.e. 0, 1, 2, 3, 4, 5, 6, 7, 8 and 9. When we arrive at 9 counting up, the next number is represented by placing a 1 one place to the left and a 0 to the right of it, giving

10

Here the 1 represents the number of tens I have; in other words, this can be read as *one* ten plus *zero*, or ten. We've created a new column to the left that can be used to count tens. So now we can represent numbers above ten, such as the following:

17, which can be read as *one* ten plus *seven* (seventeen)

20, which can be read as *two* tens plus *zero* (twenty)

and so on.

Activity 31 (self-assessment)

(a) How would 53 be read using the system discussed above?

(b) What is the largest number that can be represented in this way (using two columns and ten possible digits)?

— five tens plus three

— ninety-nine

If I want to count numbers beyond ninety-nine then I need another column to the left in which to represent the number of hundreds – one hundred being the next number after ninety-nine. I can extend this system indefinitely by simply adding columns to the left: thousands, ten thousands, hundred thousands and so on. Each column has ten times the value of the column to its right. It can help to visualise the columns set out as follows.

The fact that $10^0 = 1$ was mentioned in Session 3.

Ten thousands	Thousands	Hundreds	Tens	Units
10 000	1000	100	10	1
$= 10 \times 10 \times 10 \times 10$	$= 10 \times 10 \times 10$	$= 10 \times 10$		
$= 10^4$	$= 10^3$	$= 10^2$	$= 10^1$	$= 10^0$

You can see that there are different ways in which you can think of the value of each column. For example, the ten thousands column counts how many 10 000s (or how many 10^4s) there are in a number. Using the exponent form can provide a helpful shorthand.

So, for example, the numbers 98 503, 350 and 1 could be represented as follows.

Ten thousands, 10 000	Thousands, 1000	Hundreds, 100	Tens, 10	Units, 1
9	8	5	0	3
0	0	3	5	0
0	0	0	0	1

As I've said, each column value (or *weighting* as I will call it) in this table is found by multiplying the weighting to the right by 10. The first weighting (on the far right-hand side) is 1.

The fact that in this system ten digits (0 to 9) are used, with each column value being found by multiplying the weighting to the right by 10, leads to it being called a *base 10 numbering system* or a *decimal numbering system*. Using base 10 we can count to, and write down, any number we want. In fact, the decimal system started as a result of people using ten fingers to count.

Numbering systems that work in this way, using a set of digits or symbols and weighted columns, are called *place value systems*. Not all numbering systems are place value – Roman numerals, for instance. Systems such as the Roman system make arithmetic very difficult indeed; try adding XVIII to MCVI if you want to see what I mean. But that's another story, and one that is well outside the scope of this module!

6.2 Other bases

The decimal numbering system, based on ten digits, is not the only way in which to count and do arithmetic. I can use any base, providing I have enough symbols to represent the individual digits. For example, if I choose base eight (usually referred to as the *octal system*) then I am using the digits 0 to 7 and my table of columns begins as shown below, with each column weighting being eight times the weighting of the column to the right. Note that the first weighting is again 1 – this is the case for any place value system.

Five hundred and twelves	Sixty-fours	Eights	Units
512 $= 8 \times 8 \times 8$ $= 8^3$	64 $= 8 \times 8$ $= 8^2$	8 $= 8^1$	1 $= 8^0$

In the context of the octal system, when I write

73

this doesn't mean seven lots of *ten* plus three, as it would in the decimal system; instead it means seven lots of *eight* plus three. You can see this by positioning the digits of the octal number in the table.

Five hundred and twelves, 512	Sixty-fours, 64	Eights, 8	Units, 1
0	0	7	3

So the octal number 73 is equivalent to the decimal number $7 \times 8 + 3$, i.e. 59.

As you can see from this, unless we indicate clearly which system we're working in there may well be confusion. A common way to do this is to use a subscript to indicate the base. So I would write 73_8 to mean the octal number 73.

Activity 32 (self-assessment)

(a) What does it mean to write $73_8 = 59_{10}$?

(b) What decimal number is 2341_8 equivalent to? You may wish to use a calculator for this part of the activity.

Activity 32 showed you how to convert an octal number to a decimal number. It's perfectly possible to do the conversion the other way round, finding the octal number equivalent to a decimal number – but I won't pursue this here.

I can extend the method used here to develop any number base system that I choose. However, if I go beyond base 10 then I will need more symbols for my digits. For instance, you might come across the hexadecimal system, which uses base 16. In order to have enough symbols, it uses A, B, C, D, E and F to represent 10, 11, 12, 13, 14 and 15

The Babylonians had a numbering system that used base 360; this required 360 different symbols.

respectively. Base 16 is useful in some branches of computing because $16 = 2^4$, and powers of 2 are useful in computing in the same way that powers of 10 (10, 100, 1000, etc.) are useful when counting money.

6.3   Base 2: binary numbers again

You've seen that using any number as a base, it is possible to create a system whose numbers are equivalent to those in the decimal system we use every day. Using 2 as the base has particular relevance to computers.

Activity 33 (self-assessment)

What digits are involved in the base 2 numbering system?

As the answer to Activity 33 shows, the numbers of the base 2 numbering system are strings of the digits 0 and 1: 11001011, for example. This should look familiar! Base 2 numbers are the binary numbers you encountered in Session 5.

You saw in Session 5 how computers can store binary numbers. Now you can also begin to see how computers use binary numbers to represent the decimal numbers we use in everyday life.

For the binary number system the table of columns begins as follows.

Eights	Fours	Twos	Units
8	4	2	1
$= 2 \times 2 \times 2$	$= 2 \times 2$		
$= 2^3$	$= 2^2$	$= 2^1$	$= 2^0$

Activity 34 (self-assessment)

What would be the weightings of the next three columns to the left?

Binary to decimal

A table such as the one above can be used to convert binary numbers to their decimal equivalents in just the same way as you saw for octal numbers. Below, for example, I've positioned two binary numbers, 1001_2 and 111_2, in the table.

> Note the use of the subscript 2. You should omit the subscript only if the context makes clear which number base you are working in.

Eights, 8	Fours, 4	Twos, 2	Units, 1
1	0	0	1
0	1	1	1

For each binary number, I multiply each digit in each column by the weighting at the head of that column to yield a decimal number. Adding these decimal numbers together produces a decimal number equivalent to the binary number I started with. So for 1001_2 I have:

$1 \times 8 = 8$

$0 \times 4 = 0$

$0 \times 2 = 0$

$1 \times 1 = 1$

Adding these numbers together gives $8 + 0 + 0 + 1 = 9$, so $1001_2 = 9_{10}$. In other words, I've found out that the binary number 1001 is equivalent to the decimal number 9.

Activity 35 (self-assessment)

(a) Try this procedure with the second number in the table, 111_2.

(b) Convert the following binary numbers to their decimal equivalents.

  (i) 10_2

  (ii) 10001_2

  (iii) 11000_2

  (iv) 11111_2

There is potential for confusion when speaking about numbers with different bases. The number 10_2 should never be referred to as ten. It is best to say either 'one zero' or 'binary two'.

'There are 10 types of people in the world, those who understand binary numbers and those who don't.'
Anon

Decimal to binary

So far you've learned how to convert a binary number into its decimal equivalent. But, of course, to represent decimal numbers in binary form on a computer requires a conversion the other way round. That is, it's necessary to find the binary equivalent of a decimal number.

There is a procedure for converting from decimal to binary that relates to the tables you have seen above. First I write down the weightings for each column, from right to left, up to the largest value that does not exceed the decimal number I am converting. So, for example, if I am converting 157 to binary then I start by writing the following.

256	128	64	32	16	8	4	2	1

Activity 36 (self-assessment)

What would be the number in the next column to the left? Why do I stop at 128?

Now I subtract the weighting 128 from 157 and place a 1 in the 128 column. This gives a remainder of 29. The table expresses the fact that $157 = 1 \times 128 + 29$.

128		64	32	16		8	4	2	1
157 − 128 = 29									
1									

Now I think about the remainder, 29. I move along the columns to the right until I find a weighting that can be subtracted from 29 without leaving a negative remainder. Since 64 is too large to subtract from 29, I place a 0 in the 64 column. Likewise 32 is too large to subtract from 29, so I also place a 0 in the 32 column. I can subtract 16 from 29, with remainder 13, so I place a 1 in the 16 column. The table now expresses the fact that $157 = 1 \times 128 + 0 \times 64 + 0 \times 32 + 1 \times 16 + 13$.

128		64	32	16		8	4	2	1
157 − 128 = 29				29 − 16 = 13					
1		0	0	1					

The remainder is 13. Again, I move along the columns to the right. I can subtract 8 from 13, with remainder 5, so I place a 1 in the 8 column. The table expresses the fact that $157 = 1 \times 128 + 0 \times 64 + 0 \times 32 + 1 \times 16 + 1 \times 8 + 5$.

128		64	32	16		8		4	2	1
157 − 128 = 29				29 − 16 = 13		13 − 8 = 5				
1		0	0	1		1				

The remainder is 5. I can subtract 4 from 5, with remainder 1, so I place a 1 in the 4 column. The table expresses the fact that $157 = 1 \times 128 + 0 \times 64 + 0 \times 32 + 1 \times 16 + 1 \times 8 + 1 \times 4 + 1$.

128		64	32	16		8		4		2	1
157 – 128 = 29				29 – 16 = 13		13 – 8 = 5		5 – 4 = 1			
1		0	0	1		1		1			

The remainder is 1. I can't subtract 2 from 1, so I place a 0 in the 2 column. I can subtract 1 from 1, with remainder 0, so I place a 1 in the 1 column and I am finished. In its final form, the table expresses the fact that $157 = 1 \times 128 + 0 \times 64 + 0 \times 32 + 1 \times 16 + 1 \times 8 + 1 \times 4 + 0 \times 2 + 1 \times 1$.

128		64	32	16	8	4	2	1
157 – 128 = 29				29 – 16 = 13	13 – 8 = 5	5 – 4 = 1		1 – 1 = 0
1		0	0	1	1	1	0	1

I can now read off the column entries to find that the binary equivalent of the decimal number 157 is 10011101. So $157_{10} = 1001\ 1101_2$.

> Note that you could check the answer here by starting from the binary number $1001\ 1101_2$ and converting it – using the technique you practised earlier – to its decimal equivalent. You should arrive back at the decimal number 157.

Large binary numbers are often written in groups of four digits to help with readability. Although the term is rarely used, a set of four bits (or half a byte) is called a *nibble*.

When converting from decimal to binary you don't have to give tables at each intermediate step as I've done above. You can simply show your working (the remainders) within one table. Try this in the following activity.

Activity 37 (self-assessment)

In the table below I've started the conversion process for the decimal number 178. Complete the table and write down the equivalent binary number.

128	64	32	16	8	4	2	1
178 – 128 = 50							
1							

Activity 38 (self-assessment)

Convert the following decimal numbers to binary.

(a) 199

(b) 64

(c) 328

(d) 1000

Activity 39 (exploratory)

When convenient, please go to the 'Study resources' page on the TU100 website and find the Sense activities section. Locate the Sense activity associated with this part and follow the instructions given.

6.4 Measuring data storage

When I discussed prefixes in Session 3, the examples I chose were of computer speed. You learned, for example, that a megaflop represents a speed of 10^6 – a million – floating-point operations per second.

You've seen that computers store data in bits, and I've explained that a byte is the term used for 8 bits. Computer memory is often specified in terms of bytes; for example, you might hear of a device with a memory capacity of 512 megabytes. Following the speed examples, you might reasonably think that this means the device can store 512×10^6 or 512 000 000 bytes in its memory. However, the computing and telecommunication industries don't use terms such as kilo and mega consistently.

Activity 40 (exploratory)

If you have a calculator to hand, calculate the values of 2^{10} and 2^{20}.

Comment
$2^{10} = 1024$ and $2^{20} = 1048\ 576$.

I think you'll admit that these values are temptingly close to 1000 and 1000 000, or 10^3 and 10^6.

Given the discussion above, it's not too surprising that when talking about storing data (which, after all, is done using binary numbers), the industry often uses the term kilobyte (KB) to mean 1024 bytes and the term megabyte (MB) to mean 1048 576 bytes. Note the capital K denoting 2^{10}, as opposed to the lower-case k that stands for 10^3. (Oddly, for data *transmission* as opposed to *storage* the industry uses 1000 and 1000 000 for kilo and mega respectively – and, just to add a further complication, gives quantities in bits rather than bytes.)

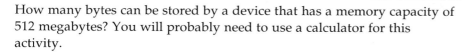

Activity 41 (self-assessment)

How many bytes can be stored by a device that has a memory capacity of 512 megabytes? You will probably need to use a calculator for this activity.

6.5   Conclusion

In the previous session you learned how an analogue quantity such as temperature can be represented digitally as a sequence of values – typically, ordinary (decimal) numbers. In this session I went on to show you how decimal numbers can be represented in binary form, so that they can be stored and manipulated inside a computer. The combination of these two ideas is where the power of computers lies: in the ability to represent the many analogue aspects of our real world – temperatures, images, sound, etc.

This session should have helped you with the following learning outcomes.

• Explain the concept of a number base.

• Convert between decimal numbers and binary numbers.

• Work with number bases.

• Perform simple calculations relating to computer memory.

• Run a simple Sense program.

Summary

In this part, 'Anything, anywhere', I started by looking at early computers and what they did. You saw that over time computers have become smaller, more numerous, more interconnected and more portable. I considered how the concept of computing is increasingly moving away from the image of one person working on their machine to that of computers being all around us, embedded in all sorts of devices and machines: truly inside anything, anywhere.

I also looked at some aspects of what happens inside a computer. You learned about the fundamental idea of using binary numbers to code digital representations, and how binary numbers can be stored inside a computer. I showed you how temperature can be represented digitally, and how decimal numbers can be represented in binary form and hence by a computer.

From your work on this part you should be able to appreciate, in outline, how various kinds of information can be represented inside a computer. For example, consider a simple document that contains only text – characters such as are on this page. Since the set of characters is discrete, each one can be represented by a binary number. A document, then, can be represented by a string of binary numbers in a computer.

In the next part you will go beyond the internal world of computers to discover how documents on the Web are created and displayed.

Activity 42 (self-assessment)

As for all the parts in this block, you should now complete the learning outcomes activity described in the *TU100 Guide*. You'll find an electronic version of the activity table used there in the 'Study resources' section on the left-hand side of the TU100 website. Download and complete that document for Block 1 Part 2, following the instructions in the *TU100 Guide* (which are repeated in the downloadable file).

No answer is provided for this activity, as your response will be unique to your background and experience of TU100 so far.

Before you move on from this part, you should ensure that you have investigated the links related to Block 1 Part 2 that are provided on the TU100 website. Then you can start Part 3, which is presented wholly online.

Answers to self-assessment activities

Activity 4

(a) The power consumption of the electric iron is 1 kW = 1 × 1000 W = 1000 W.

The power consumption of the electric kettle is 2 kW = 2 × 1000 W = 2000 W.

(b) The electric kettle and electric fire use the most power, 2000 W each; the electric iron is next at 1000 W.

(c) The electric kettle, fire and iron are all designed to produce heat.

Activity 5

The power consumption of the ENIAC was 170 kW. The power consumption of an electric fire is 2 kW. To find out how many times greater the power consumption of the ENIAC is than that of the electric fire, we divide the former by the latter:

170 kW / 2 kW = 85

When I do a calculation such as this one, in which I'm interested in proportions, it always involves dividing one by the other. Such a proportion can be expressed instead as a *ratio*. So I could have asked 'What is the ratio of the power consumption of the ENIAC to that of an electric fire?'. In that case I would write the answer as the ratio 85:1, which is read as 'eighty-five to one'.

Activity 7

(a) Generation 1: valves.

Generation 2: transistors.

Generation 3: pre-microprocessor integrated circuits.

Generation 4: microprocessors.

(b) Each successive generation of computers required less energy for a given task, and became faster, smaller and cheaper to use and to manufacture in large numbers.

Activity 8

(a) In the third generation, individual components such as transistors were integrated into an integrated circuit.

In the fourth generation, the components of the CPU were integrated into a microprocessor.

(b) Integration might result in reduced flexibility because computer manufacturers can no longer access individual components that have been integrated. This means that only the available 'off the shelf' configurations can be used. So unless there is high demand for a particular configuration, it's unlikely that it will be available.

Activity 10

(a) 1965 was during the third generation (which was founded on the invention of the integrated circuit).

(b) The move from the third to the fourth generation was led by development of the microprocessor – an integrated circuit containing the CPU.

Activity 12

Consider the number of grains on each square.

- The first square contains 1 grain of rice.
- The second square contains 2 grains of rice – 2 multiplied by 1, or 2.
- The third square contains 4 grains of rice – 2 multiplied by itself twice or 2×2.
- The fourth square contains 8 grains of rice – 2 multiplied by itself three times, or $2 \times 2 \times 2$.
- The fifth square contains 16 grains of rice – 2 multiplied by itself four times, or $2 \times 2 \times 2 \times 2$.

By now you can probably spot the pattern. If we consider the nth square, where n is any number from 2 to 64, the number of grains of rice on that square is 2 multiplied by itself $n - 1$ times.

So the number of grains of rice on the 21st square is 2 multiplied by itself 20 times.

Activity 13

$16 = 8 \times 2$, so 16 years is 8 lots of 2 years.

After 8 lots of 2 years, the number of components in an area that originally contained one component would be 2^8.

$2^8 = 2 \times 2 \times 2 \times 2 \times 2 \times 2 \times 2 \times 2 = 256$.

So the answer is 256 components.

Activity 14

$2^6 = 2 \times 2 \times 2 \times 2 \times 2 \times 2 = 64$.

$2^9 = 2 \times 2 \times 2 \times 2 \times 2 \times 2 \times 2 \times 2 \times 2 = 512$.

$10^3 = 10 \times 10 \times 10 = 1000$.

$10^4 = 10 \times 10 \times 10 \times 10 = 10\,000$.

$8^3 = 8 \times 8 \times 8 = 512$.

You may have noticed that 2^9 and 8^3 have the same value. This is because $8 = 2 \times 2 \times 2$, so $8 \times 8 \times 8$ is the same as $(2 \times 2 \times 2) \times (2 \times 2 \times 2) \times (2 \times 2 \times 2)$.

Activity 15

(a) $10^5 = 10 \times 10 \times 10 \times 10 \times 10 = 100\,000$.

(b) The pattern is that 10^n is 1 followed by n zeros.

(c) $1000\,000$ is 1 followed by 6 zeros. So $1000\,000 = 10^6$.

Activity 16

The prefix 'kilo' indicates 1000, which is 10^3.

Activity 20

Here is my list.

- I was woken by my digital alarm clock – that's one.
- I drove my car. In doing this I must have interacted with about 20 computers – they would have been involved in everything from using the accelerator to climate control, changing gear and listening to the radio.
- I swiped my gym card for access to the gym; this has a barcode that is scanned electronically, and then the data is read into a computer.
- I bought petrol. There was certainly one computer associated with the pump, not to mention the credit card transaction, which probably triggered several others at my bank.
- I stopped at the ATM for cash – that's at least one – but the ATM must have contacted my bank, so that's two at least, and I'm ignoring all the computers on the network between the two.
- I used my mobile phone – that's probably more than one in itself, but then there are the embedded systems in the phone network to consider and the phone of the person I'm calling … I'm guessing, but maybe 10 or so in total.
- I swiped my ID card to get into the office: a couple there.
- I checked my electronic diary for appointments.
- In my office, I researched material for TU100 on the Web, which involved maybe 10 servers for each search and 50 searches – say 500 altogether.
- When I bought lunch the till was electronic, but I won't count this since I didn't use it directly.
- Oh, then there's my PC and laptop …
- I microwaved my supper, so that's another one at least.

I make that 542 computers in total, but you can see that the numbers are really quite vague. To be honest, I have no idea how many computers I used while carrying out many of the above activities. For example, when

I was searching on the Web I could easily have used many times the 500 servers I've quoted.

Activity 21

Figure 29 shows the detailed timeline I drew up.

Activity 23

Here are the drawbacks I identified.

1   Technical problems in the cloud, such as network disruptions, may make data or services unavailable.

2   Data may be insecure: depending on the country in which it is stored, your data might be released without your knowledge to that country's authorities.

Activity 24

There are 8 three-bit binary numbers in total: 000, 001, 010, 011, 100, 101, 110 and 111.

Activity 25

I'd be able to form $2^8 = 256$ binary numbers.

Activity 27

I would say that quantities 2, 3, 4 and 6 are definitely analogue (although, as you will see later, we might choose to measure them with discrete instruments). Quantities 1 and 5 are discrete.

Activity 28

Analogue representations can take any value within a range. They represent analogue quantities. Temperature, for example, can be converted into an electrical 'analogue' that shows the same pattern of variations as in the measured temperature.

In a digital representation, a limited set of values is used to represent the original quantity. So a digital representation can take only certain values. Digital representations may be used to represent both discrete and analogue quantities. Morse code is an example of a digital representation of a discrete quantity; the numerical display of a digital thermometer is an example of a digital representation of an analogue quantity.

Activity 29

There are many examples you might have come up with. For instance:

*   A digital clock provides a digital representation of time, which is an analogue quantity.

*   The speed of a car – an analogue quantity – might be displayed using a digital speedometer.

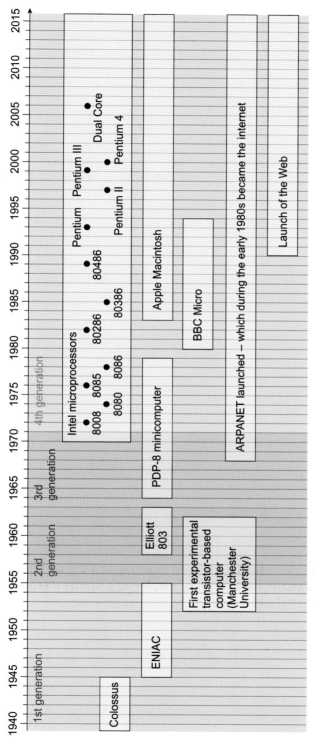

Figure 29   A more detailed version of the timeline from Figure 18

Activity 30

(a) One byte is 8 bits. So I can represent 2^8 or 256 different binary numbers, and hence 256 different discrete values.

(b) Yes. For each degree from 1 to 99 I need two values if I'm to measure to half a degree accuracy; for example, 22.0 °C and 22.5 °C. So I need $99 \times 2 = 198$ values plus another one to represent 100, giving 199 in total. Since one byte gives me 256 values, I can do it with 57 values to spare.

If I wanted more accuracy then I would need to use more bits to represent values, but given enough bits I would be able to represent any required degree of accuracy.

Activity 31

(a) *Five* tens plus *three* (fifty-three).

(b) Ninety-nine (99).

Activity 32

(a) This means that the octal number 73 is equivalent to the decimal number 59, which is what I showed in the example.

(b) To work this out, I first place the digits of this octal number in the table.

Five hundred and twelves, 512	Sixty-fours, 64	Eights, 8	Units, 1
2	3	4	1

From this I can see that $2341_8 = (2 \times 512 + 3 \times 64 + 4 \times 8 + 1 \times 1)_{10} = 1249_{10}$.

Activity 33

The digits 0 and 1.

Activity 34

The next column weighting is two times the value of the last column weighting, i.e. 2×8 or 2^4 or 16.

The column weighting after that is two times this last value, i.e. 2×16 or 2^5 or 32.

The column weighting after that is two times this last value, i.e. 2×32 or 2^6 or 64.

Activity 35

(a) For 111_2 I have the following from the table:

$1 \times 4 = 4$

$1 \times 2 = 2$

$1 \times 1 = 1$

So $111_2 = (4 + 2 + 1)_{10} = 7_{10}$.

(b) (i) $10_2 = 2_{10}$

  (ii) $10001_2 = 17_{10}$

  (iii) $11000_2 = 24_{10}$

  (iv) $11111_2 = 31_{10}$

Activity 36

The next number in the series is 256, which would exceed 157, so I stop at 128.

Activity 37

128		64	32		16		8	4	2		1
$178 - 128 = 50$			$50 - 32 = 18$	$18 - 16 = 2$					$2 - 2 = 0$		
1		0	1		1		0	0	1		0

The table shows that the decimal number 178 is equivalent to the binary number 1011 0010.

Note that it is important to write down the final 0. The binary numbers 10110010 and 1011001 are not the same (you can check this by working out the decimal equivalent of 1011001 – it is not 178!). This is just as with decimal numbers where, for example, the numbers 23 and 230 are not the same.

Activity 38

(a) 1100 0111

(b) 100 0000

(c) 1 0100 1000

(d) 11 1110 1000

Activity 41

$512 \times 1048\ 576 = 536\ 870\ 912$ bytes.

Glossary

analogue   A term used to refer to a quantity that can take any value in a continuous range of values.

analogue representation   A representation of an analogue quantity in which the representation varies continuously with the quantity. Based on the word 'analogous'.

application   A piece of software designed to carry out a particular set of tasks for the user, e.g. word processors and spreadsheets.

axis   The horizontal or vertical scale on a graph or chart.

binary logic   A system invented by George Boole in which 1 represents TRUE and 0 represents FALSE. Also known as *Boolean logic*.

binary number   A sequence of digits, each of which is either 1 or 0.

bit   A digit in a binary number when stored in a computer.

byte   A set of eight bits.

calm technology   A form of ubiquitous computing in which technology supports our daily activities but is more or less imperceptible.

CD/DVD drive   A device that reads from and writes to CDs/DVDs.

central processing unit (CPU)   The command centre of a computer system that interprets and executes program instructions, and controls system input and output and the storage and retrieval of data. Also known as the *central processor*.

cloud computing   A method of using remote computers to process and store data and run applications.

data   The sets of numbers, letters or symbols used for processing by a computer.

decimal numbering system   A system of numbers that uses ten digits (0 to 9) and weighted columns where each column value is ten times the one to its right. Also known as the *base 10 numbering system*.

digital representation   A representation that portrays a quantity as a sequence of discrete values such as 1, 2, 3 or 00, 01, 10.

discrete   A term used to refer to a quantity that varies in a series of steps or jumps, or that can have only one of a finite set of values.

electronic switch   An electronic component that can take one of two states, on or off.

embedded computer   A computer designed to perform one or more specialised tasks as part of another device that might contain electrical and mechanical components. Generally embedded computers do not allow new programs to be loaded and run, and they can be accessed only by interacting with the device they have been embedded into.

exponential growth   Growth in which each value is a fixed multiple of the previous value.

exponential notation   The use of numbers involving exponents or powers, e.g. 2^3.

floppy disk   A small, plastic, magnetic storage medium.

graphical user interface (GUI)   An interface based on graphical representations of objects in a computer system, which are manipulated using pointing and gesture-based devices.

graphics   The pictorial representation of data by a computer.

hard disk drive   A persistent storage medium in which data is written to and read from a rapidly rotating magnetic disk. Also known as a *hard drive* or a *hard disk*.

integrated circuit (IC)   A miniaturised electronic circuit whose components have been etched using photographic techniques onto a sheet of semiconductor such as silicon. Also known as a *chip, microchip* or *silicon chip*.

killer app   An application that entices people into buying a particular computer.

logarithmic   A term used to describe a graph that has a logarithmic scale along one of its axes.

logarithmic scale   A scale on which the increments increase in multiples of a constant amount.

main memory   The internal memory of a computer system – temporary storage areas for programs and data. Usually takes the form of semiconductor memory chips commonly known as **random-access memory (RAM)**.

mainframe   A very large, expensive computer designed to perform high-speed, reliable computation. The name 'mainframe' comes from the frame-like cabinets in which such computers were originally housed. Mainframes are usually installed in purpose-built rooms with specialised power and air-conditioning systems.

memory   The part of a computer system that stores programs and data while they are waiting to be executed by a CPU.

microcomputer   An early personal computer, also known as a *micro*.

microprocessor   A specialised later development of a single integrated circuit that contains a computer's central processing unit and is capable of performing computations.

minicomputer   A computer originating in the second generation, typically equipped with several monitors and keyboards.

Moore's law   The prediction (related to one made by Gordon Moore in 1965) that the density of components in an integrated circuit would double every two years.

multi-user computer   A computer whose resources can be accessed simultaneously by several users.

peripheral device   Any device, either internal or external, that is not part of the motherboard, e.g. hard drive, monitor, printer. Also known simply as a *peripheral*.

personal computer (PC)   A small computer, usually intended for a single user, based on a microprocessor.

power   (1) In physics, the rate of flow of energy, measured in watts. (2) A term used in mathematics to indicate a number to which another number is raised. In the expression 10^2 the number 2 is the power. Also known as an *index* or *exponent*.

random-access memory (RAM)   Memory that holds data only while it receives power; when power is removed the content of the memory is lost. The term 'random-access' signifies that direct access to any location in memory is possible, as opposed to serially addressable memory – that is, it takes the same amount of time to access data held in any location in memory.

supercomputer   A type of mainframe distinguished by the highest processing speeds, often used for scientific work such as simulations of nuclear explosions, weather forecasting and aerospace development.

terminal   A monitor and a keyboard, connected to a computer by telephone lines, used for data entry and display.

transistor   A crystal of silicon that can act as a switch. Transistors work in a very similar way to valves.

Turing test   A test for identifying artificial intelligence, suggested by Alan Turing.

ubiquitous computing   An area of computer science that is interested in the development and implementation of computer technologies when they have been integrated into everyday objects and environments. Also known as *ubicomp*, *everyware* or *pervasive computing*.

valve A glass vacuum tube that can act as a switch.

web server A computer on the internet that responds to requests for web pages.

workstation Similar to a personal computer, but much more powerful and usually networked for many users.

References

Clarke, A.C. (1945) 'V2 for Ionosphere Research?', Letters to the Editor, *Wireless World*, February, p. 58.

Giles, K. and Hedge, N. (1994) *The Manager's Good Study Guide*, Milton Keynes, The Open University.

Moore, G.E. (1965) 'Cramming more components onto integrated circuits', *Electronics*, vol. 38, no. 8, 19 April.

Thompson, B. (2008) 'Storm warning for cloud computing', *BBC News* [online], 27 May, http://news.bbc.co.uk/1/hi/technology/7421099.stm (accessed 17 May 2010).

Weiser, M. (1996) *Ubiquitous Computing* [online], http://www.ubiq.com/hypertext/weiser/UbiHome.html (accessed 17 May 2010).

Weiser, M. and Brown, J.S. (1996) *The Coming Age of Calm Technology* [online], Palo Alto, CA, Xerox PARC, http://nano.xerox.com/hypertext/weiser/acmfuture2endnote.htm (accessed 17 May 2010).

Acknowledgements

Grateful acknowledgement is made to the following sources.

Text
Box 3: Thompson, B. (2008) 'Storm warning for cloud computing',
http://news.bbc.co.uk/1/hi/technology/7421099.stm

Figures
Figure 2: © http://en.wikipedia.org/wiki/
File:NAMA_Machine_d'Anticythère_1.jpg, Creative Commons Licence

Figure 4: © Bletchley Park Trust/SSPL via Getty Images

Figure 8(b): © IBM

Figures 9(a) and 9(b): Courtesy of Dave Phillips

Figure 10: © Google Inc.

Figure 11: © Cray Inc.

Figure 17: © Sweetym/iStockphoto

Figure 23: © Jeff Hower/iStockphoto

Figure 25: © Steve Goodwin/iStockphoto

Figure 26: © Tom Hahn/iStockphoto

Part 3
Building the Web

Author: Neil Smith

You can find this part of the block online. A link is provided on the TU100 website.

Part 4

Geography is history

Author: David Chapman

You can find this part of the block online. A link is provided on the TU100 website.

Part 5

Seeing Sense

Authors: Mike Richards and Rob Griffiths

This part of the block gives you an introduction to programming using Sense and the SenseBoard. Further details are provided in the resources page associated with this part on the TU100 website.

Part 6

Wireless communications and mobile computing

Author: Arosha Bandara

You can find this part of the block online. A link is provided on the TU100 website.